A Swift Pair of Messengers

Also by Bhikkhu Sujato through Santipada

A History of Mindfulness
How tranquillity worsted insight in the Pali canon

Beginnings
There comes a time when the world ends...

Sects & Sectarianism
The origins of Buddhist schools

Bhikkhuni Vinaya Studies
Research & reflections on monastic discipline for Buddhist nuns

Dreams of Bhaddā
Sex. Murder. Betrayal. Enlightenment. The story of a Buddhist nun.

White Bones Red Rot Black Snakes
A Buddhist mythology of the feminine

A Swift Pair of Messengers

Calm with insight in the Buddha's words

BHIKKHU SUJATO

SANTIPADA

Originally published by Inward Path Publishers in 2001.
Revised edition published in 2012 by Santipada.
This edition published in 2017 by Kamma Mountain Ltd.

ISBN 978-1-921842-00-9

Typeset in Skolar using LꞋATEX.

Contents

Introduction

'Wide open are the doors to the deathless!
Let those with ears to hear make sure their faith!'

—THE BUDDHA, MN 26.21

WITH THIS INSPIRED VERSE the Buddha declared that the freedom he had realized was available to all. Nothing less than escape from death itself was his promise, and this goal was available to anyone willing to listen to his message with a sincere and confident heart. Many teachers had appeared before him—as they still do today—with such extravagant claims. But the distinctive feature of the Buddha's teaching was a pragmatic course of spiritual training leading step by step to the goal.

This work is an attempt to clarify the meaning and function of *samatha* (tranquility) and *vipassanā* (insight) in Buddhist meditation. Much has been written on this topic, yet a cloud of confusion persists. Though modern Buddhism claims to rest on a foundation of inquiry, many meditators seem willing to invest their spiritual trust in meditation techniques without carefully considering exactly what it is they are practicing.

3   This is not a beginner's introduction nor a guide to the nuts and bolts of practice. It is intended for those who have some knowledge and experience in Buddhist meditation, but who are confused by the diverse and often conflicting opinions expressed by meditation teachers. All of those teachers, however, are unanimous on one point—the greatest Teacher, the Teacher of teachers, is the Buddha himself. We wish to follow the path of the Buddha, so our starting point should be to see what the Buddha himself said, and did not say, about meditation. Even though the main aim here is theoretical clarity, I hope to offer inspiration and practical tools for meditation as well.

4   The sutta passages are the heart of this essay. I obviously have my own views on this matter, and offer explanations accordingly, but you should accept these only to the extent that they aid your understanding of the suttas.

5   We should never forget the chasm that lies between the label, the word, and the experience to which it points. Even a simple notion, such as 'Swan River', is so far from capturing the reality of the thing itself: the brackish, lazy smell; the waters filled with jellyfish; or the absence of actual swans. Still worse, the word drags in a welter of *others*, unseen rivers and unnoticed allusions. And if something so banal is so fraught, what then the hope for agreement in matters such as these, anciently subtle and yet intensely, immediately personal? My only comfort is that the Buddha himself, having briefly flirted with such doubts, decided that words could be good enough.

6   It is the dedicated thirst for understanding, not the complacent acquiescence in an ancient theory, which gives rise to true wisdom. All too often Buddhists come out trumpeting their commitment to free inquiry over tradition, then

content themselves with critiquing any tradition but their own. Really embodying the Dhamma requires a creative engagement with the teachings.

7   In this work, I hardly address the question of how best to apply these teachings in a modern context. While individuals will come to different solutions, I believe that a sincere response will not be easy or comforting; it will not prop up our complacent existence, but will sweep out our stays, precipitating a radical realignment of lifestyle.

8   If we are to understand samādhi, we must first consider how it works within the context of the path as a whole. The most fundamental division of the path is threefold: virtue, samādhi, and understanding. Each of these works to purify and develop the mind in essential ways, working from the coarse to the refined.

9   All Buddhist practice is based on ethical conduct. Virtuous ethical conduct dams the poisonous outflow of defilements which pollute behavior of body and speech, corrupting an individual's relations with the world outside. It conduces to peace and harmony in relationships, in society, and in nature, for a moral person acts in a responsible, cooperative, and non-afflictive manner.

10   The mind established on ethics will lean towards peace, and yet ethics alone is not sufficient to bring true wisdom. For that, we need the specialized development of consciousness through meditation, which the Buddha called *samādhi*. Samādhi clarifies the still waters, cleansing the subtle afflictions that pollute the mind, cloud the emotions, and darken wisdom. It leads to peace and harmony in the world within, with each mental factor functioning appropriately, in balance and unity.

11 · And in these still waters, understanding can clear up the source of suffering once and for all. As the Buddha said, over and over again, in his final days, as the great message he wished to be remembered for:

12 'Samādhi imbued with virtue is of great fruit and benefit. Understanding imbued with samādhi is of great fruit and benefit. The mind imbued with understanding is completely released from all poisons, that is, the poisons of sensual pleasures, existence, and ignorance.'[1]

13 Meditation is the key to liberating insight. In fact the exalted mind states of samādhi, when used as a basis for insight, are the very doors to the deathless.

14 'What, Bhante Ānanda, is one principle declared by the Blessed One who knows and sees, arahant, and fully enlightened Buddha whereby for a monk abiding diligent, ardent, and resolute the unreleased mind becomes released, the unevaporated poisons become evaporated, and the unattained supreme security from bondage becomes attained?'

15 'Here, householder, a monk, quite secluded from sensual pleasures, secluded from unbeneficial qualities, enters and abides in the first jhāna... second jhāna... third jhāna... fourth jhāna... the heart's release through loving-kindness... the heart's release through compassion... the heart's release through admiration... the heart's release through equanimity... the base of infinite space... the base of infinite consciousness... the base of nothingness... [In all of these cases] he reflects thus: "This attainment of the base of nothingness is formed by volition and acts of will." He understands: "Whatever is formed by volition and acts of will is impermanent, subject to cessation." Standing on that, he

---

[1] DN 16.1.12

attains the evaporation of the poisons [or to the state of non-returning]. This, householder, is one principle declared by the Blessed One... whereby the unattained supreme security from bondage becomes attained.'

16   When this was said, the householder Dasama of the city of Aṭṭhaka said to Venerable Ānanda: 'Just as if, Bhante Ānanda, a man seeking one entrance to a hidden treasure were to come all at once upon eleven entrances to a hidden treasure; so too when seeking one door to the deathless I have all at once come to hear of eleven doors to the deathless. Just as if, Bhante, a man had a house with eleven doors, and if that house were to burn down he would be able to save himself through one or other of those doors; so too I will be able to save myself through one or other of the eleven doors to the deathless.'[2]

17   Samatha, or peace of mind, is a gentle and unobtrusive quality. Meek and shy, she sometimes seems unable to hold her own against the forthright boldness of her brother, vipassanā, with his claims to be the central, unique Buddhist meditation, the direct route to 'ultimate reality'. And yet she has a unique contribution to offer, no less precious for being unobvious.

18   Persistent attempts have been made to diminish the significance of samatha's role in Buddhist meditation in the never-ending search for a shortcut to happiness, so typical of our restless times. We are told that it is difficult in fast-paced modern times to find the tranquility of jhāna; which is obviously true, and yet it merely underscores how important serenity is for us, here & now. It is precisely because our postmodern world stresses the utility of analytical intelligence so excessively that the complementary holistic

---

[2]   MN 52

qualities of serenity and joy are sorely needed. Perhaps this essay may make some small contribution towards rehabilitating samatha to her rightful position as equal partner in that noblest of tasks, the development of the mind.

19   In this work the path is first examined with a comprehensive survey of core doctrinal categories, emphasizing the role of samatha. The spotlight then turns to conditionality, attempting to pin down the precise nature of the causal connection between key factors. The allimportant question, of course, is how to actually walk the path. This is therefore described next, showing the training for both monastics and laity. Given the central importance of samādhi in all the above teachings, the question naturally arises as to why it is so useful—how does samādhi work, and what do we get out of it? The highest benefit of samādhi is its support in attaining the various stages of enlightenment, and so the exploration of the path concludes by presenting the noble ones as living embodiments of the path. Lastly I consider the most important of the sutta passages which have been invoked to cast doubt on the necessity of jhāna. Issues relating to the translations have as far as possible been reserved for an appendix so as to not burden the text. A brief selection of comments by some of the most respected contemporary scholars and meditation masters is included.

20   For those who helped me bring this work to light, thank you. Special thanks are due to Ven. Brahmali, who made detailed comments on an earlier draft, some of which have substantially altered the final presentation. For the many faults which doubtless remain, I alone am solely responsible.

21   In this new edition, I have completely revised the text. The first version of this book was written when I was staying in the caves and cliffs of Ipoh, surrounded by high, inaccessible,

and forbidding walls of rock. More than a little of this found its way into the prose. I have tried to open out the text a little, simplifying some of the philosophical matter, while expanding the explanations. I have removed some of the more involved discussions on dependent origination, as they were tangential to the main argument. However, the basic structure and scholarship remains identical.

22   In the decade since I first wrote this book I have not seen any reason to change my basic position. If anything, the importance of samatha seems more obvious to me than ever, and I find myself wondering why we as a meditative tradition are still having this conversation. Things are shifting; the vipassanā rhetoric has toned down, and more teachers are teaching jhānas. Perhaps the time for this book has passed; but as long as major schools of Buddhism continue to claim that jhānas are not necessary for the Buddha's path, I think we still need to listen to what the Buddha had to say on the matter.

Chapter 1

A Handful of Leaves

And the Blessed One addressed Venerable Ānanda: 'It might occur to you: "In the past we had the guidance of our Teacher—now we have no Teacher!" But it should not be regarded thus. The Dhamma and vinaya I have taught and laid down for you will be your Teacher when I have gone.'

—The Buddha, DN 16.6.1

WHO should we believe? Amid the shifting sands of opinion, is there a solid rock of certainty on which to stand? The Buddha insisted that personal experience must be the ultimate criterion. But for the unenlightened, personal experience can be ambiguous, even misleading. To complicate matters further, in these times of information overload there is a bewildering diversity of teachers and teachings, all claiming to be based on experience.

In this work I aim to address, not the question of the Kālāmas—'How do we decide between different religious teachings?'—but rather: 'How do we decide between different interpretations of the Buddha's teachings?' This question also arose for the Buddha's followers as his life drew near its end. His answer, known as the four great references, is recorded as follows:

3 'Here, monks, a monk may say this: "Face to face with the Blessed One, friend, have I heard, face to face with him have I received this: 'This is Dhamma, this is vinaya, this is the message of the Teacher'..."

4 'Again, monks, a monk may say: "In such and such a dwelling lives a Sangha with an elder, a leader. Face to face with that Sangha have I heard: 'This is Dhamma, this is vinaya, this is the message of the Teacher'..."

5 'Again, monks, a monk may say: "In such and such a dwelling live many elder monks of much learning who have mastered the tradition, Dhamma experts, vinaya experts, systematized summary (*mātikā*) experts. Face to face with them have I heard: 'This is Dhamma, this is vinaya, this is the message of the Teacher'..."

6 'Again, monks, a monk may say: "In such and such a dwelling lives a monk, an elder, of much learning, who has mastered the tradition, a Dhamma expert, a vinaya expert, a systematized summary expert. Face to face with this elder have I heard, face to face with him have I received it: 'This is Dhamma, this is vinaya, this is the message of the Teacher'..."

7 [In all of the above cases:] 'Monks, the speech of that monk should neither be delighted in nor disparaged. Every word and phrase should be well apprehended, placed beside the sutta and compared with the vinaya. Should they not fit in with the sutta or accord with the vinaya, you should conclude: "Certainly this is not the word of the Blessed One, and has been wrongly apprehended by that elder." Thus, monks, you should reject it. If they fit in with the sutta and accord with the vinaya, then you should conclude: "Certainly this

is the word of the Blessed One, and has been rightly apprehended by that elder.'"[1]

8   It seems that the Buddha, though aware of the possibility of breakdown in transmission, nevertheless trusted the Sangha to adequately preserve his teachings. The suttas offer the seeker a unique opportunity to engage with a direct expression of perfect enlightenment. Lucid, immediate, and pragmatic, this Dhamma emerged at a time when experiments in democracy could form a model for organization of the Sangha; when freedom of religious creed and practice was unquestioned; and when the religious establishment was straining under the weight of the rituals, hierarchies, and mystifications of age-old tradition, unable to address the issues most relevant to people's lives. The spirit of inquiry responded to these conditions with a bewildering diversity of religious sects, of which the Buddha's best stood the test of time.

9   The universal, timeless quality of the Buddha's words, like an arrow aimed straight at the heart of the human condition, inspired an unprecedented effort to preserve his Teachings 'for those who feel'.

10   The following passage clarifies both what the Buddha meant by 'sutta' and why this standard is important.

11   'In future times there will be monks undeveloped in bodily conduct, virtue, mind, and understanding... when suttas spoken by the Tathāgata are taught—profound, profoundly meaningful, transcendental, dealing with emptiness—they will not listen, they will not lend an ear, they will not set their minds on profound knowledge, they will not think those teachings worth apprehending and mastering. But when suttas com-

---

[1]   AN 4.180; DN 16 4.8–4.11

posed by literati are taught—literary, with fancy wordings, fancy phrasings, irrelevant, spoken by disciples—they will listen, they will lend an ear, they will set their minds on profound knowledge, they will think those teachings worth apprehending and mastering.

12   'Thus, monks, from corrupt Dhamma comes corrupt vinaya; from corrupt vinaya comes corrupt Dhamma. This is the fourth danger as yet unarisen, which will arise in the future. Be alert, and strive to abandon it.'[2]

13   The texts relied on here are the only ones considered authoritative by all schools of Buddhism. My intention is to establish an interpretation of the crucial features of the path acceptable to all Buddhists by not relying on later authorities peculiar to any particular school. These texts are the five Nikāyas of the Pali Sutta Piṭaka—excluding later additions to the fifth Nikāya such as the Paṭisambhidāmagga—together with the Vinaya Piṭaka. There are, no doubt, some extraneous additions even within this limited body of texts; yet such additions are mainly limited to supplementary matter, such as narrative backgrounds and legends, and do not substantially affect the doctrine. The Vinaya Piṭaka as a whole is later than the Suttas, but it still contains some early material. However this is only occasionally relevant for meditation studies.

14   These Nikāyas correspond to the Āgamas preserved in various Indic languages, as well as the Chinese and Tibetan traditions. A thorough comparative study of the meditation material in all these texts still remains to be done. I have not done such a study, and do not attempt any but the most perfunctory comparative inquiries in this work. Nevertheless, in the years since writing the first edition of this book I have

---

[2]   AN 5.79

studied in some detail the meditation material in different traditions. I have not found any major variations; such differences as I have noticed tend, if anything, to reinforce the perspective I arrived at in this book. Some of the main results of those comparative studies are included in my book *A History of Mindfulness*.

15   I don't want this to become a 'fundamentalist' critique of contemporary schools of meditation or of the traditional commentaries. It seems that the commentaries in particular have become a favorite target of criticism, particularly for Western scholars. This might be influenced by the generally odious image of institutionalized medieval monasticism in the West. But time and again initially plausible critiques turn out to be shortsighted, and, worse, the critics then proceed to make as many or more new blunders. In fact the commentaries are an invaluable mine of information on Dhamma, Pali, history, and much else, and any translator owes them a great debt. However, I am resolutely committed to interpreting the suttas on their own terms, and try as I might to see the matter from the commentarial position, I have in several instances reached conflicting conclusions. I have noted some important points of divergence; the points of agreement are too many to mention. I have mentioned such differences, not out of desire to criticize, but because the commentarial system is highly influential in contemporary meditation circles and therefore has a direct effect on people's lives. I believe that a careful appraisal of the tradition in the light of the suttas will facilitate appreciation of its true value.

16   I have yet to see any satisfactory study along historical and comparative lines of the development of Theravādin thought in these issues. I may simply add that the commen-

taries universally praise jhāna and devote great lengths to explain what it is and how to develop it. However, certain variations in their explanations of key points suggest that the commentaries themselves, as compilations of the opinions of various teachers, contain some divergence of opinion.

17 Thus 'purification of mind' is defined in the Dīgha Nikāya commentary as 'the thoroughly mastered eight attainments [i.e. form and formless jhāna] as a basis for vipassanā', but in the Visuddhimagga it is 'the eight attainments together with access [samādhi]'. Again, where the Visuddhimagga treats 'mind' as both absorption and access samādhi, the Saṁyutta Nikāya commentary to the same verse defines 'mind' simply as 'the eight attainments'. Again, 'momentary samādhi' occurs only twice, both times subordinate to jhāna, in the Visuddhimagga, but more often and with more independence in its commentary.

18 These differences could be explained away as mere variations in the letter; but the natural conclusion in the face of the evidence is that there is a divergence in meaning, perhaps a historical development. Far from being a uniform emanation of enlightened wisdom, the commentarial literature is a complex and evolving scholasticism. The tradition itself is quite happy to chronicle unreconciled differences of opinion. In any case, the task I have set myself is to explain what the suttas say, and so I have throughout avoided relying on the commentaries. Nor, with two slight exceptions, have I relied on the testimony of contemporary meditators, as such testimony is diverse and unverifiable.

19 A problem can arise: since even learned scholars can disagree on the meaning of sutta passages, is the above standard any use? Of course we can never hope for complete

agreement. Any text admits of multiple possible readings. This is all the more so since we are missing so much background and context for the suttas. Nevertheless, two related principles of interpretation can help clarify obscure passages. One we call the principle of proportion, the second, the principle of historical perspective.

The Principle of Proportion

20 The principle of proportion involves assessing the relative importance and reliability of sutta passages using a variety of acceptable objective criteria. If there are any gray areas, anomalies, or possible conflicts, then the more important and reliable passage should take precedence. It is not necessary to assume that there either are or are not contradictions in the sutta texts as we have them, nor that the secondary passages are not authoritative, simply that the primary passages should be granted greater authority.

21 Consider how the suttas were assembled. First, the Buddha would have taught; his followers would memorize the teachings and later embed them in a framework of time and place. This indicates that it is the doctrinal teachings themselves, rather than background details or anecdotes, which should be accorded greater weight. This can be shown by comparing the following two passages, each introducing the same sutta, the Sāmaññaphala. The first is from the Vinaya Cūḷavagga, recounting the history of the recitation of the suttas and vinaya by the Sangha after the Buddha's passing away.

22   'Ānanda, where was the Sāmaññaphala spoken?'
23   'At Rājagaha, Bhante, in Jīvaka's mango-grove.'
24   'Who with?'

25   'With Ajātasattu Vedehiputta.'

26   Thus Mahā Kassapa asked Ānanda about the setting and the individuals. Using the same method, he
asked about the five Nikāyas and Ānanda answered
each question.[3]

27   From the Sāmaññaphala Sutta as recorded in the Dīgha
Nikāya:

28   Thus have I heard. At one time the Blessed One was
living near Rājagaha, in the mango-grove of Jīvaka
Komārabhacca, together with a great Sangha of twelve
hundred and fifty monks. Now at that time Ajātasattu,
the king of Magadha, was seated on the upper veran-
dah of his palace, it being the full moon observance
day of the fourth month, the Komudi, surrounded by
his ministers.[4]

29   Although the story is essentially the same, the form is
different and many details have been added. Even the words
'Thus have I heard' are missing from the Cūḷavagga account.
From other contexts it is clear that that the phrase 'Thus have
I heard' is reserved for relating events second-hand.[5] If one
was actually present, the phrase 'Face to face have I heard it'
is used instead. 'Thus have I heard' therefore would not have
been spoken by Venerable Ānanda, since he was present
when many of the suttas were delivered. It must have been
inserted by later redactors, specifically to acknowledge the
fact that they are passing down material that they did not
learn directly from the Buddha.

30   The Buddha described his teaching as the 'suttas spoken
by the Tathāgata', and it seems from the above account that
his early disciples also regarded the 'sutta' in the most au-

---

[3]   Vin Cv 11.1.8
[4]   DN 2.1
[5]   MN 127.17; DN 5.21

thoritative sense as the doctrinal teachings spoken by the Buddha (or his enlightened disciples), as distinct from the incidental details of where it was spoken and to whom, etc.

31   We should also bear some other common sense considerations in mind when interpreting the suttas. Minor teachings should concede precedence to central and important themes, especially those given special significance by the Buddha himself. Poetry is naturally less suited to precise and detailed exposition of doctrinal points than prose; in addition, much of the poetry of the Tipiṭaka seems to be of later date than the prose. When quoting verses, therefore, we will try to restrict ourselves to the earlier strata. Similes, inferences, and passages of dubious or controversial interpretation are likewise of secondary consideration.

32   For several centuries the suttas were handed down orally, most reciters concentrating on learning texts from a single Nikāya. The arrangers of the suttas would naturally wish to edit their material so that the core teachings would be found in each Nikāya, the fifth (minor) Nikāya being only somewhat of an exception. In this way by learning one Nikāya one should be able to come to an accurate understanding of all the major teachings. The Nikāyas differ in perspective and emphasis, but not in doctrine. The interesting conclusion follows that it is unlikely that a text crucial for deciding an important doctrinal point would be found in only one or two Nikāyas.

33   The Buddha clearly felt that at least some of his discourses stood in no need of interpretation.

34   'These two misrepresent the Tathāgata... one who shows a sutta whose meaning requires further explanation as not requiring further explanation; and one

who shows a sutta whose meaning does not require further explanation as requiring further explanation.'[6]

35   There is therefore no justification for the modern Theravādin assertion that the suttas teach only a provisional, conventional teaching, which the abhidhamma explains in terms of ultimate reality; both of these methods are found within the suttas themselves. The suttas are full of similes, parables, and brief or enigmatic teachings which require interpretation. Sometimes the Buddha would do so, or encourage a disciple to do so. Often it is up to the audience, the Buddha apparently recognizing that the process of sincere investigation into meaning can be of more value than being handed all the answers on a plate. But definitive statements of central doctrinal importance belong to those statements that are fully explained. Care should be taken, therefore, to avoid imputing unjustified meanings to such passages.

36   So what then are these central teachings on practice? On the internal evidence of the texts themselves, I would suggest that there are three teaching frameworks that should be regarded as primary.

37   The first is a set of seven groups of Dhammas, later known as the thirty-seven wings to enlightenment, which are taught frequently in the suttas, and which the Buddha shortly before he passed away described as the teaching which 'should be cultivated, developed, and made much of, so that this holy life will last long, for the benefit and happiness of many people, out of compassion for the world, for the benefit and happiness of deities and humans.'[7]

38   The second teaching framework is less well known, but should be seen as central since it is a practical application

---

[6]   AN 2.3
[7]   DN 16.3.50

of dependent origination. It is said that who sees the Dhamma sees dependent origination, and who sees dependent origination sees the Dhamma; the fundamental significance of causality in the Buddha's teaching is underlined by the famous verse of Venerable Assaji, regarded as the ideal epitome of Dhamma.

39

> 'Whatever phenomena arise from a cause —
> Their cause and their cessation.
> Such is the doctrine of the Tathāgata
> The Great Contemplative.'[8]

40   For the teachings where dependent origination is applied to the way of practice, I use the term 'dependent liberation'.

41   Finally, the Buddha said that practice in this teaching is gradual, with no sudden penetration to knowledge; this gradual training comprises the heart of the second to twelfth suttas in the Dīgha Nikāya and many others.

42   These three teachings — the wings to enlightenment, the dependent liberation, and the gradual training — are discussed in chapters 3, 4, and 5.

43   This then is the first principle for interpretation, the principle of proportion, which we are proposing as a reasonable guideline to resolve conflicts in doctrinal understanding. Can we really suppose that the Buddha would have left a crucial question underpinning the whole way of practice to a background story, minor category, or dubious inference? Surely it is more reasonable to suppose that he would have described the way of practice very carefully, defined his terms clearly, and repeated them often. This being so, when faced with gray areas or unclear passages, we should interpret the minor statements so as to agree with the major statements, not the other way around.

---

8   Vin Mv 1.23

The Principle of Historical Perspective

44   Our second interpretative guideline is the principle of historical perspective. In the 2,500 years since the Buddha, discussion, systematization, and perhaps modification of the meaning of what he said has continued unabated. It is quite inappropriate to read terminology and concepts of a later era into the texts of an earlier era. This error may occur in a number of ways: new terminology may be invented for old ideas; old words may acquire new meanings; or completely new concepts may be invented and artificially imposed on the old texts.

45   Remember that in the text quoted at the beginning of this paper the Buddha conferred sole authority on the sutta and vinaya; no abhidhamma and certainly no commentaries. The abhidhamma did not exist in the Buddha's lifetime, but, along with some later works included in the suttas, was developed during a period of approximately four centuries after the Buddha's passing away. The commentaries were not finalized until 1,000 years after the Buddha, over the same period when the Mahāyāna Sūtras were composed.

46   Some say that even if these texts did not exist in their present form, still their essence was spoken by the Buddha and his disciples. This claim, while not altogether baseless, is misleading. Much of the material in the abhidhamma and commentaries is perfectly in accord with the suttas and may well be descended from sayings of the Buddha. However, much of their teachings are radically different in both form and content from the suttas, and it is precisely these passages which give rise to controversy.

47   We can, fortunately, sidestep the question of whether these teachings differ only in the letter or also in the mean-

ing as a strictly separate and secondary issue. The first of the great references quoted above refers to a teaching that a monk claims to have heard from the Buddha's lips; even this must only be accepted if it is in line with the suttas and vinaya. So the suttas can simply be taken on their own terms, and for all important matters they should be sufficient. To hold that the Buddha was unable to explain what he meant in a central question regarding the path to Awakening would be a curious aspersion on his ability.

48   So what are these later teachings? The Theravāda tradition has coined a range of terms and concepts which, although unknown to the suttas, constitutes the standard vocabulary of contemporary Buddhist meditation teachings. These include 'momentary' and 'access' samādhi; 'vipassanā jhāna', 'samatha jhāna', and 'transcendental jhāna'; the 'one whose vehicle is serenity' and the 'one whose vehicle is pure (or dry) insight'. So prevalent is the influence of these terms that the conception of the path of meditation they imply is tacitly accepted by almost all books on meditation, and has been 'authorized' by inclusion in standard reference works. Someone interested in Buddhist meditation can pick up a wide variety of books from diverse sources, simple and complex, all of which re-affirm the same ideas. The plain fact that these special concepts are based on scholastic writings dated centuries after the Buddha and peculiar to the Theravāda school is obscured.

49   If we wish to understand the suttas as those who listened to them, we must first carefully examine the contextual significance of crucial terms. Sound textual analysis must proceed from unambiguous contexts as a basis for inferring the meaning of ambiguous contexts. Any interpretation which

relies on reading non-standard meanings into ambiguous passages should be rejected out of hand.

Samādhi

50   *Samādhi* is a regular synonym for 'one-pointedness of mind' (*cittekaggatā*) or 'unification' (*ekodibhāva*). Both '*samādhi*' and 'unification' occur in the formula for the second jhāna, while elsewhere 'one-pointedness' is also said to already occur in first jhāna.[9] The verb forms of 'unification' (*ekodihoti* or *ekodikaroti*), which regularly occur alongside *samādhiyati*, may also refer to first jhāna.[10] Here is a standard definition of *samādhi* from the suttas:

51   'One-pointedness of mind with seven [path] factors as requisites is called noble right *samādhi* with its vital conditions and requisites.'[11]

52   Right *samādhi*, or one-pointedness of mind in the context of the path, is the four jhānas.[12] We shall see below that whenever *samādhi* is explicitly defined in core doctrinal categories, it is always the four jhānas.

53   This is by far the most important meaning of *samādhi* in the suttas. Nevertheless, it is possible, with a little hunting, to find cases which suggest *samādhi* can have a broader meaning.

54   In a very few contexts the meaning, not clarified by the context, may be jhāna, or possibly mere 'concentration' in

---

[9]   MN 43.20 (quoted at ch. 3.70), MN 111.4

[10]   SN 40.1, MN 12.7. The absence of these terms in the normal formula for the first jhāna seems to imply a certain reservation over whether first jhāna is fully one-pointed or not, no doubt due to the continued operation of initial & sustained application of mind.

[11]   DN 18.27, MN 117.3, SN 45.28, AN 7.42

[12]   DN 22.21, etc. (quoted ch. 3.15).

the ordinary sense of the word.[13] One passage speaks of a monk establishing the 'mind one-pointed in *samādhi*' while in all four postures, including walking.[14] This would seem to be difficult to square with the usual understanding of jhāna, although it would not necessarily directly contradict anything in the suttas. Everything else in this sutta, though, is quite standard—virtue, abandoning the hindrances, energy, mindfulness, bodily tranquillity (which strikes me as slightly odd in the context of walking), and *samādhi*, with a verse extolling both samatha and vipassanā. Perhaps we might suspect some slightly clumsy editing; and we should not forget the many times when the meditator sits down cross-legged before entering *samādhi*.

55   More often, *samādhi* is used to describe meditative states of vipassanā or liberation. These include three of the four kinds of 'development of *samādhi*',[15] the 'basis of reviewing',[16] and the 'signless heart-*samādhi*'.[17] These are not substitutes for jhāna in any important doctrinal categories; in fact, they regularly follow *after* jhāna. It may be noted that 'development' (*bhāvanā*) often refers not to the basic establishing of a meditation subject, but to its further, advanced development.[18] Presumably, establishing one-pointedness in jhāna enables the mind to maintain a comparable level of one-pointedness in the more complex task of vipassanā, justifying the term *samādhi*.

---

[13] Vin Cv 5.3, AN 5.29, AN 5.151 (quoted ch. 8.33).

[14] AN 4.12

[15] DN 33: 1.11, AN 4.41

[16] AN 5.28

[17] DN 16.2.25, MN 121.11, MN122.7, SN22.80, SN 40.9, SN 43.12.6–8, SN 41.7, AN 7.53, cp. MN 43.7*ff*.

[18] E.g. MN 44.12

56   Very rarely, *samādhi* is used of a state of meditation that may precede jhāna. The following unique passage describes such a pre-jhanic *samādhi*.

57   'For a monk devoted to the higher mind, there are coarse taints—misconduct of body, speech, and mind. The aware and competent monk abandons, dispels, eradicates, and annihilates them.

58   'When they are abandoned... there are middling taints—thoughts of sensual pleasures, ill will, and cruelty...

59   'When they are abandoned... there are subtle taints—thoughts of family, country, and reputation. The aware and competent monk abandons, dispels, eradicates, and annihilates them.

60   'When they are abandoned and eradicated, from there on there remain only thoughts about Dhamma.[19] That *samādhi* is not quite peaceful, nor refined, nor possessed of tranquillity, nor unified, but is actively controlled and constrained. There comes a time when the mind is steadied within, settled, unified, and concentrated in samādhi. That *samādhi* is peaceful, refined, possessed of tranquillity, unified, and is not actively controlled or constrained.

61   One can incline the mind to witness with direct knowledge whatever principle can be witnessed with direct knowledge, and become an eye-witness in every case, there being a suitable basis.'[20]

62   It is only when the *samādhi* is 'peaceful and refined', in other words real *samādhi*, that it leads to the fruits of practice. These higher attainments of the path are regularly said

---

[19] 'Thoughts about the Dhamma' means just that. The commentary asserts that the phrase refers to the ten 'taints of vipassanā'. But not only is this an anachronistic reading of a later concept into an earlier text, the context has nothing to do with vipassanā. Cp. AN 5.73, Iti 3.86.

[20] AN 3.100

to be the outcome of jhāna, so in such contexts it is only reasonable to infer that *samādhi* here means jhāna, as usual.[21] Until the minor hindrances have been fully overcome, and the mind stops thinking, even 'thinking about the Dhamma', the mind cannot enter jhāna and realize the deeper insights.[22] The only significance of pre-jhānic *samādhi* is to precede true *samādhi*, and hence it is ignored in all expositions of right *samādhi*.

Jhāna

63   According to the Pali Text Society's *Pali-English Dictionary*: '[*Jhāna*] never means vaguely "meditation". It is the technical term for a special religious experience reached in a certain order of mental states. It was originally divided into four such states.' This unambiguous meaning occurs many hundreds of times.

64   If one searches among the thousands of early Buddhist texts, it is possible to find a few different usages. Very rarely, for example, *jhāna* may refer to a non-Buddhist form of self-torment such as the 'breathless *jhāna*'.[23]

65   In prefixed form, *jhāna* often means 'ponder', 'brood'. Occasionally the simple and prefixed forms are used together in a disparaging sense. Despite the obvious incongruity, I

---

[21] E.g. DN 1.1.31, DN 6.6, AN 6.26, AN 6.61. See too the bases for psychic power discussed in ch. 3.225*ff*.

[22] In speaking of the obstacles to meditation the passage only mentions *particular* subtle taints, and so it—probably deliberately—does not quite clarify whether the '*samādhi*' accompanied by 'thoughts about Dhamma' is totally free of hindrances or not—there is no mention of sloth & torpor, etc. We might surmise that hindrances, even if not actually arisen, may re-emerge at any moment due to the lack of one-pointedness, which is the defining characteristic of true *samādhi*.

[23] MN 36.21*ff*.

retain the word 'jhāna' in the following passages for the sake of consistency.

66   'Then, when Māra Dūsī had possessed the brahman householders, they abused, reviled, mocked, and harassed the virtuous monks of good character thus: "These baldies, monkies, menial darkies spawned from the Ancestor's feet, claim: 'We're doing *jhāna*! We're doing *jhāna*!' and with shoulders drooping, heads hanging, and all limp they do *jhāna*, re-do *jhāna*, out-do *jhāna*, and mis-do *jhāna*. Just like an owl on a branch watching out for a mouse... like a jackal on a riverbank watching out for fish... like a cat by a door-post or a dustbin or a drain watching out for a mouse... like a clapped-out donkey hanging around a door-post or a dustbin or a drain does *jhāna*, re-does *jhāna*, out-does *jhāna*, and mis-does *jhāna*..."'[24]

67 It hardly needs to be said that this kind of *jhāna* is not what the Buddha was encouraging his followers to practice! Nevertheless, this passage provides a clue as to the basic, non-specialized meaning of jhāna: close, sustained, concentrated observation at a single point.

68 The significant image of 'food' as the object of *jhāna* recurs in the following remarkable passage, which encompasses the broadest range of meaning of 'jhāna'.

69   'Sandha, you should practice the *jhāna* of the thoroughbred steed, not the *jhāna* of the clumsy nag. What is the *jhāna* of the clumsy nag?

70   'The clumsy nag, when tied up by the feeding trough, does *jhāna* thus: "Fodder! Fodder!" For what reason? It does not occur to him: "What task will the trainer set for me today? What can I do for him in return?" Tied up by the feeding-trough, he just does *jhāna* thus: "Fodder! Fodder!" In just the same way, a certain clumsy

---

[24] MN 50.13; cp. MN 108.26–27, quoted ch. 3.74–75).

nag of a person who has gone to a forest, the root of a tree, or an empty place, abides with heart obsessed and overwhelmed with sensual lust... ill will... sloth & torpor... restlessness & remorse... doubt. He does not understand the escape from these things in accordance with reality. Having formed these things inside himself, he does *jhāna*, re-does *jhāna*, out-does *jhāna*, and mis-does *jhāna*. He does *jhāna* dependent on earth... water... fire... air... the base of infinite space... the base of infinite consciousness... the base of nothingness... the base of neither perception nor non-perception... this world... the world beyond... on what is seen, heard, sensed, cognized, attained, sought out, and explored by the mind. This is the *jhāna* of the clumsy nag of a person.

71 'What is the *jhāna* of the thoroughbred steed?

72 'The excellent thoroughbred steed, when tied up by the feeding-trough, does not do *jhāna* thus: "Fodder! Fodder!" For what reason? It occurs to him: "What task will the trainer set for me today? What can I do for him in return?"... The excellent thoroughbred steed regards the application of the whip as a debt, imprisonment, loss, and misfortune. In just the same way, the excellent thoroughbred steed of a person... does not abide with heart obsessed with the five hindrances... He does not do *jhāna* dependent on earth... on what is seen, heard, sensed, cognized, attained, sought out, and explored by the mind. And yet he does practice *jhāna*.'[25]

73 This passage brings out a number of points in the usage of the term '*jhāna*'. The similes differentiate between the mind focused on one thing and the mind engaged in reflective consideration—the former is called '*jhāna*', the latter not. The series of four derivatives of '*jhāna*' augmented with pre-

---

[25] AN 11.10

fixes is always used in connection with the five hindrances, never with the four *jhānas*. The mention of the four elements seems to be an idiomatic reference to the four 'form' *jhānas*. To preserve consistency, the text applies *jhāna* to the formless attainments—a common usage in later literature but perhaps unique in the suttas. The '*jhāna*' mentioned in the final phrase may be the fruition attainment of arahantship. Notice that this meditative experience of enlightenment is distinguished from the form and formless *jhānas*.

74   Although the text does not unequivocally praise *jhāna*, it is not the *jhāna*, but the person practicing it, who the Buddha criticizes, and then only by comparison with the arahant. As we shall see below, the ideas of 'food' and 'dependence' imply dependent origination; so all conditioned states are being faulted here from the standpoint of ultimate wisdom as being still bound up with rebirth. It should be re-emphasized that these broad usages of the term *jhāna*—here mentioned for completeness—are exceedingly rare.

75   These are the only meanings of the words *jhāna* and *samādhi* which can be unambiguously established from the early suttas. Since these two words occur so often with such clear meaning, it seems reasonable to assume that they refer to the four jhānas unless there is contextual evidence otherwise. As samādhi may have a broader meaning on occasion, however, we will try to confirm the contextual meaning whenever possible.

Vipassanā jhāna

76   The controversial term *vipassanā jhāna* seems to stem from a historical development in the application of the terms 'samatha' and 'vipassanā'.

77   In the suttas, no meditation technique is labeled, such as by saying 'kasiṇas and loving-kindness are samatha, satipaṭṭhāna is vipassanā'. A growing tendency to segregate and systematize the various meditation subjects developed into the prevailing practice of identifying samatha and vipassanā with the meditation subjects themselves, rather than with the mental qualities which the techniques foster. Having thus labeled a certain technique as 'vipassanā', it was found that experiences of rapture, serenity, and bliss occur during 'vipassanā'. These experiences were then called *vipassanā jhāna*.

78   But these emotional qualities are precisely what 'samatha' refers to. This is not some new kind of 'jhāna' happening in 'vipassanā', it is just samatha pure and simple. It simply happens to occur while practicing a meditation technique whose primary purpose is to develop vipassanā.

79   One may hear that 'vipassanā' helps to relieve stress, solve psychological imbalances, or increase compassion; but these things are aspects of samatha, 'development of the mind', regardless of the label stuck on the technique. As long as the mind is still moving, however, and as long as the five external senses still impinge, it falls short of true jhāna— the mind absolutely content to rest still within itself.

Transcendental jhāna

80   There is one further concept to be discussed: 'transcendental jhāna' (*lokuttarajjhāna*), which has been pressed into service as a substitute for 'samatha jhāna' to fulfil the path factor of right samādhi. This idea is based on the Paṭisambhidāmagga, one of the latest books in the Sutta Piṭaka, as well as the canonical Abhidhamma texts. It was taken up

and developed by the commentators using their own special concepts.

According to the developed commentarial theory, 'transcendental jhāna is a special kind of jhāna which occurs only at the time of penetrating to the noble paths and fruitions. This samādhi can apparently occur with the same mental factors as any of the four jhānas, but is distinguished by taking Nibbana as its object and by permanently eradicating, rather than merely suppressing, the defilements appropriate to each path. The four paths are each conceived as lasting one 'mind moment'[26]—another commentarial concept—occurring once only, while the fruition can be re-entered by the noble ones after appropriate preparation. This 'path-moment' is supposed to last less than a billionth of the duration of a flash of lightning.[27]

With the possible exception of fruition attainment,[28] none of these ideas finds support in the suttas. Supporters of the theory will usually point to the Mahācattārīsaka Sutta, which distinguishes between the transcendental and non-transcendental path for the first five path factors. However the text does not maintain that distinction for the factors of the samādhi aggregate.[29] The divergence in presentation is not arbitrary. The express purpose of the sutta is to show how all the path factors function to support samādhi for one developing the noble path. The first five factors are accord-

---

[26] See Vsm 22.15ff.

[27] For a detailed exposition, see Dr Henepola GUNARATANA, *A Critical Analysis of the Jhānas in Theravāda Buddhist Meditation.*

[28] Some such attainment seems to be attested to, for the arahant at least, by a number of passages, of which we have met one above. These passages, however, fall well short of justifying all the details of the commentarial theory. A detailed discussion of the fruition falls outside the scope of this essay on the path.

[29] MN 117

ingly given special definitions appropriate in the context of
samādhi. In particular, right view and right intention are
defined by way of cognitive function rather than objective
content. But the final three factors in their normal formu-
lation already pertain directly to samādhi, so stand in no
need of any special definition here. In any case, the mere
mention of the words 'noble, poison-free, transcendental, a
factor of the path' even if they were applied to jhāna would
hardly imply the details of the commentarial theory.[30]

83   The definition of the spiritual faculty of samādhi is also
relied on to support this thesis. In the section dealing with
the spiritual faculties I offer an alternative interpretation,
reserving a technical critique of the commentarial position
to Appendix A.

84   On these insubstantial grounds rests the entire elaborate
edifice of the commentarial theory. One may wonder why
the Buddha, normally so precise in wording, would choose
to use such terms as 'path' and 'person' to describe a 'mind-
moment'. Such ideas may have evolved from the recorded
instances of apparently sudden penetration to the Dhamma.
It seems that the path is entered at one time, developed gradually, and matures into the fruition at another time, after a
short or long interval.[31] This is explained with such similes
as chicks breaking out of their shells after incubation, or
the collapse of a ship's rigging after rotting away for a long
time in the weather.[32]

85   The commentarial notion that the 'path' happens in a flash-
ing moment, and that therefore all passages that refer to the

---

[30] See e.g. DN 28.18. At AN 5.79 quoted above, the suttas themselves are
said to be 'transcendental' (*lokuttara*).
[31] See Vin Pj 4.3
[32] SN 22.101

'path' in its technical sense refer to that moment only, is a curious idea indeed, and one that finds no support in the suttas. On the contrary, the suttas constantly speak of one on the path as a person who develops the path over a period of time. Key sutta passages on the path are collected below.

86   'Just as, monks, this great ocean deepens gradually, inclines gradually, slopes gradually, with no abrupt precipice, even so in this Dhamma-vinaya there is gradual training, gradual work, gradual practice, with no abrupt penetration to profound knowledge.

87   ... 'Just as the great ocean is the home of many great beings... so too this Dhamma-vinaya is the home of many great beings: the stream-enterer, the one on the way to witnessing the fruit of stream-entry [and so on.].'[33]

88   'As he develops samatha prior to vipassanā, the path is born in him. He cultivates, develops, and makes much of that path.'[34]

89   'One who, regarding the well-taught word of Dhamma,
            Lives on the path, restrained and mindful
        Cultivating blameless states—
            This is the third kind of monk, the liver of the path.'[35]

90   'The four pairs of people, the eight individuals, these are the Sangha of the Blessed One's disciples: worthy of gifts, worthy of hospitality, worthy of offerings, worthy of reverential greeting, an unexcelled field of merit for the world.'[36]

91   'Those eight people who are praised
            The four pairs of the Blessed One's disciples
            They are worthy of offerings

---

[33] AN 4: 200–1 cp. Vin Cv 9.1.4, Ud 5.5
[34] AN 4.170
[35] Snp 88
[36] DN 16: 2.9 etc.

What is given to them bears great fruit.'[37]

92   'An offering to one on the way to witnessing the fruit
of stream-entry can be expected to repay incalculably;
what could I say of an offering to a stream-enterer?'[38]

93 The Dhamma-follower and faith-follower are those who
are on the way to stream-entry. For the commentaries they
are merely a 'mind-moment', yet the suttas constantly treat
them as a 'person' in the ordinary sense.

94   'He is incapable of doing any action having done
which he would be reborn in hell, the womb of an
animal, or the ghost realm. He is incapable of passing
away without witnessing the fruit of stream-entry.'[39]

95   'Just as that tender calf just born, being urged on
by its mother's lowing also breasted the stream of the
Ganges and got safely across to the further shore, so
too those monks who are Dhamma-followers, faith-
followers—by breasting Māra's stream they too will
get safely across to the further shore.'[40]

96   'What do you think, Bhaddāli?... Suppose there was
a monk who was a Dhamma-follower... a faith-follower,
and I told him: "Come, monk, be a plank for me to walk
across the mud." Would he walk across himself, or
would he dispose his body otherwise, or would he say
"No"?'

97   'No, Bhante.'[41]

98   'When that venerable one makes use of suitable
dwellings, associates with good friends, and composes

---

[37] Snp 227
[38] MN 142.6
[39] SN 25
[40] MN 34.10
[41] MN 65.11

his spiritual faculties, he may witness... the supreme goal... He still has work to do with diligence.'[42]

99 In the following passage, one of the chief lay disciples relates how he learns of the monks' attainments.

100 'It is no surprise, Bhante, when the Sangha is invited by me, that deities approach and tell me: "That monk, householder, is one released on both sides; that one is released by understanding; that one is a personal witness; that one has attained to view; that one is faith-released; that one is a Dhamma-follower; that one is a faith-follower; that one is virtuous, of good qualities; that one is immoral, of evil qualities." '[43]

101 Seeing some wanderers of other sects walk by, King Pasenadi asks the Buddha:

102 'Bhante, are those among those in the world who are arahants or attained to the path to arahantship?'[44]

103 'It is hard, Great King, for you as a lay person enjoying sensual pleasures, dwelling crowded by children, using sandalwood imported from Benares, wearing garlands, perfume and make-up, and accepting gold and money, to know whether these are arahants or those attained to the path to arahantship.'[45]

104 Or similarly, in speaking of what kind of monks would attend an animal sacrifice, the Buddha said:

---

[42] MN 70.21–22, cp. AN 7.53

[43] AN 8.22

[44] We might note here that the word 'path' (*magga*) is rarely used in the suttas to denote those developing the path; the synonym 'way' (*paṭipadā*), defined just as the noble eightfold path (SN 45.31) is the usual term. Nor is the path normally divided into four as such; the path is just the noble eightfold path, but those at different stages practice for different immediate goals. This being so, the phrase 'the path to arahantship' simply refers to the eightfold path.

[45] SN 3.11

105   'Neither arahants nor those attained to the path to
        arahantship will attend such a sacrifice. Why not? Be-
        cause beatings and throttlings [of sacrificial animals]
        are seen there. But arahants or those attained to the
        path to arahantship will attend the kind of sacrifice
        where regular family gifts are specially given to virtu-
        ous monks.'[46]

106   Those of us who cannot imagine a 'mind-moment' lying in
      the mud or attending a meal or accepting a gift will conclude
      that the commentarial 'instant-path' theory cannot be relied
      on to explain the suttas.

107   The 'mind-moment' theory of the path does not merely
      conflict with a few minor passages, it is at odds with the
      very nature of samādhi as taught in the suttas. The suttas
      regularly speak of samādhi as a gradual settling of activities
      resulting in a stable coalescence of mind that lasts for a sub-
      stantial period of time, into which one 'enters and abides'.
      The word 'abides' (*viharati*) is specifically and exclusively
      used in Pali to denote an ongoing situation or event. A typical
      example:

108   'And so, Anuruddha, abiding diligent, ardent, and
        resolute I perceived limited light and saw limited forms,
        I perceived measureless light and saw measureless
        forms even for a whole night, a whole day, a whole
        night and day.'[47]

109   This then is our second principle of interpretation, that of
      historical perspective. This principle guards against playing
      'Chinese whispers' with the Dhamma, relying on an inter-
      pretation of a retelling of an exposition of a summary of
      something the Buddha was supposed to have said. The origi-

---

[46] DN 5.23 cp. Vin Mv 1.20, Ud 1.10
[47] MN 128.29

nal teachings are available to us. Great as our gratitude is to the monks who preserved and passed down the suttas, do we really suppose that any of them could explain Dhamma better than the Buddha himself? The idea that commentarial or abhidhamma concepts are needed to correctly interpret the suttas hardly accords with the Buddha's own description of his liberating teaching.

110   'Perfect in every aspect, fulfilled in every aspect, with neither lack nor excess, well explained and entirely complete.'[48]

111   In claiming that his teaching was complete, the Buddha, of course, did not pretend that he had answered all questions and given all facts. He did claim, however, to set out with sufficient detail, clarity, and precision a framework for understanding adequate to serve as guide for all essential questions of theory and practice. This is illustrated with the famous simile of the handful of leaves.

112   Then the Blessed One, taking a few *siṁsapa* leaves in his hand, addressed the monks:

113   'What do you think, monks? Which is greater, the few leaves in my hand or those left up in the trees?'

114   'The few leaves taken up by the Blessed One in his hand are less, Bhante; those left up in the trees are certainly greater.'

115   'Just so, monks, the things I have directly known but I have not declared to you are certainly greater; what I have declared is less. And why are they undeclared by me? They are pointless, not pertaining to the fundamentals of the holy life, not leading to repulsion, fading away, cessation, peace, direct knowledge, enlightenment, Nibbana. Therefore they are undeclared by me.

---

[48] DN 29.16

116   And what is declared by me? This is suffering... This
is the origin of suffering... This is the cessation of suffering... This is the way of practice leading to the cessation of suffering. And why is that declared by me?
Because it has a point, it is pertaining to the fundamentals of the holy life, leading to repulsion, fading away,
cessation, peace, direct knowledge, Nibbana. Therefore it is declared by me.'[49]

---

[49] SN 56.31

Chapter 2

Samatha & Vipassanā

'Suppose, monk, a king had a border city with strong
ramparts, walls, and arches, and six gates. The gate-
keeper there would be clever, competent, and intelligent,
and would keep strangers out but let acquaintances in. A
swift pair of messengers coming from the eastern quarter would question that gatekeeper thus: "Where, friend,
is the lord of the city?" "There he is, sirs, he is sitting
in the middle at the crossroads." Then that swift pair
of messengers would present a message in accordance
with reality to the lord of the city and leave by the way
they came. I have made up this simile to convey a meaning. And this is the meaning: "City" is a designation for
this body made up of the four great elements, produced
from mother and father, built up from rice and porridge,
subject to impermanence, to rubbing, wearing, breaking
up, and dispersal. "Six gates" is a designation for the
six internal sense bases. "Gatekeeper" is a designation
for mindfulness. "Swift pair of messengers" is a designation for samatha and vipassanā. "Lord of the city" is
a designation for consciousness. "In the middle at the
crossroads" is a designation for the four great elements...
"Message in accordance with reality" is a designation for

> *Nibbana. "The way they came" is a designation for the*
> *noble eightfold path.'*
>
> — THE BUDDHA, SN 35.245

WHEN WE INVESTIGATE THE MEANING of our meditation terminology, it is wise to proceed with a degree of
caution. We are discussing highly abstract, rarefied states
of consciousness, and such matters are not easy to pin down
with mere words. Our languages are formed from what is
around us, our concrete environment, and those things that
are of pressing relevance. Gradually words are divorced
from their concrete origins and pressed into service for
more abstract uses. This is why it is useful to consider how a
word is used in ordinary language first, where we can deter-
mine a simple meaning with a high degree of clarity, before
approaching the more subtle uses.

2   In ordinary usage, *samatha* means 'calming, settling, pacifying', for example, of disputes and litigations;[1] here the
meaning approaches 'cessation'. The means of settling disputes in the Sangha exemplify how samatha and vipassanā
work together. The disputants should come together in harmony; thoroughly examine the issues in accordance with
Dhamma; and unanimously agree on a solution. We thus
find *vipassanā* also used in a legalistic context.

3   And when Prince Vipassī was born, the divine eye
manifested to him as a result of past action, by means
of which he saw for a league all around both day and
night. And when Prince Vipassī was born, he was unblinkingly watchful, like the deities of Tavatisa. [Peo-
ple said:] 'The Prince is unblinkingly watchful', and so

---

[1]   MN 104.13

> Prince Vipassī came to be called 'Vipassī'. And then, when King Bandhumā was seated adjudicating a legal case, he sat Prince Vipassī on his lap and instructed him regarding the legal case. And Prince Vipassī, even while seated on his father's lap, having thoroughly investigated, drew a conclusion regarding the legal case by a logical method... and so Prince Vipassī was all the more called 'Vipassī'.[2]

4   Here, two aspects of vipassanā are brought forth. Firstly, the penetrative, clear-eyed observation of what is occurring in the present moment. And secondly, the ability to infer a correct conclusion by closely examining the evidence before one's eyes, understanding it in line with valid general principles.[3]

5   The precise denotation of *samatha* and *vipassanā* in the context of meditation can be derived from a passage quoted more fully below. Samatha is the steadying of the mind, its settling, unifying, and concentrating in samādhi. It is therefore similar in meaning to 'unification of mind', the most distinctive mental quality of jhāna or samādhi.[4] Vipassanā is the seeing and exploring of activities. It therefore refers to wisdom in its refined mode of investigation into the nature of reality as experience.

---

[2] DN 14.1.37. LDB is here, as all too often, thoroughly unreliable.

[3] These two aspects of vipassanā are mirrored in the context of dependent origination by 'knowledge regarding Dhamma'—understanding each factor according to the four noble truths—and 'knowledge regarding entailment'—understanding that all those who see the Dhamma, past, present, and future, will see it the same way. (SN 12.343, 12.34) Another, similar, kind of knowledge is called the 'knowledge of the regularity of natural principles'—understanding that the conditional relations between the factors always operate the same way. (SN 12.20)

[4] Cp. SN 46.51, where samatha equals 'not-many-pointedness' (*avyagga*, unscattered), an obvious synonym for one-pointedness.

6   These definitions express the quintessence of samatha and vipassanā. However, samatha and vipassanā are elsewhere treated as a comprehensive summary of the meditative aspect of the path, and the next passage treats them as leading to the development of the mind and of wisdom respectively. This implies that they may also be taken in a more general sense as including those qualities of mind leading to peace and to wisdom. They almost always occur as a pair in the suttas, and are a pair of mental qualities to be developed by means of the eightfold path.

7   'Monks, these two principles share in realization. What two? Samatha and vipassanā.

8   'When samatha is developed, what goal is achieved? The mind is developed. When the mind is developed, what goal is achieved? Lust is abandoned.

9   'When vipassanā is developed, what goal is achieved? Understanding is developed. When understanding is developed, what goal is achieved? Ignorance is abandoned.

10   'Monks, the mind tainted by lust is not released; understanding tainted by ignorance is not developed. Thus the release of heart is due to the fading away of lust; the release by understanding is due to the fading away of ignorance.'[5]

11   Sometimes the phrases 'release of heart' and 'release by understanding' denote different kinds of arahants distinguished by their giving chief emphasis to either samādhi or wisdom. Normally however, as here, they point to two complementary aspects of the release of all arahants. Thus samatha and vipassanā function as a pair, not only in the preliminary training, but also right up to the ultimate liberation. This is why the Buddha called Nibbana the 'samatha

---

[5]   AN 2:3.10

of all activities', emphasizing that samatha points to the stilling, tranquillizing, and pacifying of suffering.

12   Notice that samatha brings about the fading of lust, vipassanā the fading of ignorance. Lust is a term for the emotional aspect of the defilements; ignorance is a term for the intellectual aspect. At their most general, then, samatha may be regarded as pertaining to emotional development, vipassanā as pertaining to intellectual development.

13   The terms 'emotional' and 'intellectual' are meant here in their broadest possible connotation. By using the word 'emotional' we no more mean being moody and impulsive than by 'intellectual' we mean mere reasoning and rational thinking. Rather, we refer to that whole side of experience, half of our mind or world which deals with feelings and intuitions, the soft yin side, and that which deals with understanding and analysis, the penetrating yang side. All of us contain both of these aspects within us. Each of these aspects contains some good and some bad and must be developed in a balanced way if we are to achieve liberation—we cannot enlighten only half our mind.

14   Many similes can illustrate this mutual support. Vipassanā only is like trying to cut down a tree with a razor blade; samatha only is like using a hammer. Both together is like using a sharp axe—both penetrating and powerful. Or samatha is like the underside of a postage stamp—it sticks—while vipassanā is like the top—it informs. Or samatha is like the left foot, vipassanā like the right foot—one can only move one foot forward by leaning on the other. Or samatha is like the cool breeze at the mountain top, and vipassanā is like the view of the countryside. Or samatha is like the hand which clings to the next rung up the ladder, vipassanā like the hand which lets go of the rung below. This simile con-

tains a warning—if one lets go of both ends before reaching the top, one is likely to end up as a crumpled heap at the foot of the ladder.

15 The suttas invariably say that both samatha and vipassanā are essential and should be developed. For example, here is a sutta where Venerable Ānanda states that enlightenment must depend on some combination of samatha and vipassanā.

16 'Friends, any monk or nun who declares arahantship in my presence has arrived there by four paths or by one of them. What four? Here, friends, a monk develops samatha prior to vipassanā. While he is developing samatha prior to vipassanā the path is born in him. He cultivates, develops, and makes much of that path. As he does so his fetters are abandoned and his inherent compulsions are eradicated. Again, friends, a monk develops vipassanā prior to samatha... Again, friends, a monk develops samatha and vipassanā yoked equally... Again, friends, a monk's mind is seized by restlessness for the Dhamma. When the mind settles down within, becomes steady, unified, and concentrated in samādhi, then the path is born in him. He cultivates, develops, and makes much of that path. As he does so, his fetters are abandoned and his inherent compulsions are eradicated.'[6]

17 In this sutta, Venerable Ānanda sets out a comprehensive fourfold classification of the sequence of practice. The basic sequence is common to all four modes. First samatha and vipassanā are developed; then the path is born; then the path is developed further. The only variation is the manner of preliminary practice of samatha and vipassanā.

---

[6]   AN 4.170

18   The 'path' here is obviously the noble eightfold path. At its inception this is the way to stream-entry. This discourse says that all meditators who are to attain liberation will develop both samatha and vipassanā before becoming a noble one. Some vipassanā teachers try to interpret this passage as saying one can develops vipassanā first and then samatha (as transcendental jhāna) simultaneous with the arising of the path; or else, that one develops vipassanā until stream-entry and then samatha to support the higher stages. Neither of these readings are supported by the text, which is perfectly clear in saying both samatha and vipassanā are necessary before the arising of the noble path.

19   Let us look a little closer at how these different modes are presented in the suttas. Examples of the first mode appear frequently throughout this work, so I will leave that aside for now. Vipassanā prior to samatha is exemplified as follows. In this passage, 'imperturbable' refers to the first two formless attainments.

20   'Again, monks, a noble disciple considers thus: "Sensual pleasures... sensual perceptions... physical forms... perceptions of physical forms both here & now and in lives to come are alike impermanent. What is impermanent is not worth relishing, not worth welcoming, not worth adhering to." When he practices in this way and frequently abides thus, his mind becomes clear about this base. When there is full clarity he attains to the imperturbable now, or he decides upon understanding. With the breaking up of the body, after death, it is possible that his onflowing consciousness will pass on to the imperturbable...

21   'Again, monks, a noble disciple, gone to a forest or to the root of a tree or to an empty hut, considers thus: "This is void of a self or of what belongs to a self." When he practices in this way and frequently abides thus,

his mind becomes clear about this base. When there is
full clarity he attains to the base of nothingness now
or he decides upon understanding. With the breaking up of the body, after death, it is possible that his
onflowing consciousness will pass on to the base of
nothingness..."[7]

22   The contemplation of impermanence or not-self leads the
mind to dispassion and non-attachment. This enables the
meditator to reach the deep peace of samādhi; but this is
not the final goal, as they are still reborn.

23   The path of samatha and vipassanā yoked equally is explicitly identified in only one place.

24   'Monks, when one knows & sees in accordance with
reality the eye... visible forms... eye consciousness...
eye contact... feeling born of eye contact, then one
is not inflamed by lust for these things. When one
abides uninflamed by lust, unattached, unconfused,
contemplating danger, then the five aggregates associated with grasping are diminished for oneself in the
future, and one's craving which generates repeated
existence, accompanied by relishing & lust, delighting
here & there, is abandoned. One's bodily and mental
troubles, torments, and fevers are abandoned, and one
experiences bodily and mental bliss.

25   'Such a person's view is right view. Their intention is
right intention, their effort is right effort, their mindfulness is right mindfulness, and their samādhi is right
samādhi. But their bodily action, verbal action, and
livelihood have been well purified earlier. Thus the noble eightfold path is fulfilled for them by development
[and also the other wings to enlightenment]. These

---

7   MN 106.5, 7. Although Bhikkhu Bodhi says that fourth jhāna can be
included here as 'imperturbable', the reflection on the dangers of
physical form makes this unlikely (see MLDB notes 1000, 1007).

two qualities, samatha and vipassanā, are operating in them yoked evenly together.'[8]

26   As always, the practice requires 'right samādhi', i.e. the four jhānas.

27   In the final of Ānanda's four modes, the meditator seized by restlessness for Dhamma must turn to samatha for a cure.[9]

28   'How does he steady his mind within himself, settle it, unify it, and concentrate it in samādhi? Here, Ānanda, he enters and abides in the first jhāna... second jhāna... third jhāna... fourth jhāna.'[10]

29   This 'restlessness for Dhamma' is probably the subtle fetter of restlessness remaining to be cut by the non-returner. It seems that if this restlessness is too strong, the meditator will over-emphasize vipassanā at the expense of samatha, whereas if the corresponding 'lust for form [jhāna realms]' and 'lust for formless [jhāna realms]' are too strong, they will over-emphasize samatha at the expense of vipassanā. These imbalances must be rectified if the path is to manifest.

30   So all the four modes presented by Ānanda for realizing arahantship require harmony between samatha and vipassanā. This is simply restating a basic principle that is found time and time again in the suttas.

31   The interdependence of these two qualities is emphasized once again in the following sutta passages.

32   'A person who has samatha of the heart within himself but no vipassanā into principles pertaining to

---

8   MN 149.9-10
9   Vsm, however, identifies 'restlessness for Dhamma' with the 'taints of vipassanā' and recommends more vipassanā. See Vsm 20.106, 126f.
10   MN 122.7, cp. MN 19.8-10, MN 20, MN 4.22, SN 40.1.

higher understanding[11] should approach one who has vipassanā and inquire: "How should activities be seen? How should they be explored? How should they be discerned with vipassanā?" And later he can gain vipassanā...

33 'A person who has vipassanā into principles pertaining to higher understanding but no samatha of the heart within himself should approach one who has samatha and inquire: "How should the mind be steadied? How should it be settled? How should it be unified? How should it be concentrated in samādhi?" And later he can gain samatha...

34 'One who has neither should inquire about both [and "should put forth extreme enthusiasm, effort, endeavor, exertion, unflagging mindfulness, and clear comprehension to acquire them, just as if one's turban or hair were ablaze, one would put forth extreme effort to quench the flames"...[12]]

35 'One who has both, established in these beneficial qualities should make further effort for the evaporation of the poisons.'[13]

36 'Just as if, Nandaka, there was a four-legged animal with one leg stunted and short, it would thus be unfulfilled in that factor; so too, a monk who is faithful and virtuous but does not gain samatha of the heart within himself is unfulfilled in that factor. That factor should be fulfilled by him... A monk who has these three but no vipassanā into principles pertaining to higher understanding is unfulfilled in that factor. That factor should be fulfilled by him.'[14]

---

[11] The phrase 'pertaining to the higher understanding' doesn't necessarily imply an advanced level of vipassanā, but an understanding of impermanence, etc., rather than 'worldly' understanding of action and rebirth, etc.

[12] AN 10.54

[13] AN 4.94

[14] AN 9.4

37   So all meditators should develop both samatha and vipassanā, using a variety of strategies to overcome the diversity
of defilements.

38   'By a monk established in these five principles [that
     is: good friendship, virtue of the code of conduct, con-
     versation on Dhamma, energy, wisdom], four prin-
     ciples should be further developed: [meditation on]
     ugliness should be developed to abandon lust; loving-
     kindness should be developed to abandon anger; mind-
     fulness of breathing should be developed to cut off
     thinking; the perception of impermanence should be
     developed to eradicate the conceit "I am." '[15]

39   Bearing in mind this basic understanding of samatha and
vipassanā, we now go on to examine the three frameworks
for practice referred to above. Each of these frameworks
restates the balance and harmony between these emotional
and intellectual qualities.

40   'There's no jhāna for one without wisdom,
           No wisdom for one without jhāna;
         But for one with both jhāna and wisdom
           Nibbana surely is near.'[16]

---

[15] Ud 4.1
[16] Dhp 372

Chapter 3

The Wings to Enlightenment

> 'Those principles I have taught you having directly known them—that is, the four establishings of mindfulness, the four right efforts, the four bases of psychic power, the five spiritual faculties, the five spiritual powers, the seven enlightenment factors, the noble eightfold path—you should all train in these principles in concord, with mutual admiration, without disputing.'
>
> — THE BUDDHA, MN 103.3

THESE SEVEN GROUPS, totaling thirty-seven 'wings to enlightenment', occur frequently in the suttas, were given unique importance by the Buddha, and became a standard doctrinal framework for all schools of Buddhism. As the most important and comprehensive of these groups, we will discuss the noble eightfold path first.

The Noble Eightfold Path

2   In his first sermon, the Dhammacakkappavattana Sutta, the Buddha warned against pursuing two extremes: devotion to sensuality and devotion to self-torment. He then defined the famous 'middle way' of Buddhism which does not go anywhere near the two extremes but leads to peace, direct knowledge, enlightenment, Nibbana. This is precisely the noble eightfold path: right view; right intention; right speech; right action; right livelihood; right effort; right mindfulness; right samādhi.

3   The middleness of the middle way has nothing to do with compromise; it is not the 'mediocre' way. It is rather the way that avoids seeking for a solution to life's problems in externals, in the pleasures and pains of the body, but instead turns inwards to the peace of the mind. For this reason, the Buddha would sometimes rephrase his basic teaching on the eightfold path with the four jhānas in place of the eightfold path as a whole.

4   'Bhante, the Blessed One is not devoted to the pursuit of pleasure in sensuality, which is low, vulgar, common, ignoble, and pointless; nor is he devoted to self-torment, which is painful, ignoble, and pointless. The Blessed One is one who gains the four jhānas which constitute the higher mind, and are a blissful abiding here & now at will, without trouble or difficulty.'[1]

5   Not only here do the suttas, emphasizing that 'samādhi is the path',[2] stand jhānas in the place of the path as a whole. Even the redactors of the canon gave up trying up to enumerate all of the ways jhāna was praised by the Buddha,

---

[1]   DN 28.19 Note: this paragraph is mistakenly numbered as 20 in the PTS Pali.

[2]   AN 6.64

merely commenting: 'The collection of connected discourses on jhāna should be elaborated just as the collection of connected discourses on the path.'[3]

6   Jhāna is not merely an adornment or embellishment of the 'holy vehicle', the noble eightfold path. When the Buddha illustrated the path with the simile of a chariot, he said jhāna is the axle—the stable pivot around which the wheel revolves.[4]

7   The detailed exposition of the path is as follows.

8   'And what, monks, is right view? Knowledge of suffering, of the origin of suffering, of the cessation of suffering, and of the way of practice leading to the cessation of suffering. This is right view.

9   'And what, monks, is right intention? The intention of renunciation, of non-ill will, and of non-cruelty. This is right intention.

10   'And what, monks, is right speech? Refraining from lying, slander, harsh speech, and frivolous gossip. This is right speech.

11   'And what, monks, is right action? Refraining from killing living beings, from stealing, and from sexual misconduct. This is right action.

12   'And what, monks, is right livelihood? Here, a noble disciple, having abandoned wrong livelihood, makes his living by right livelihood. This is right livelihood.

13   'And what, monks, is right effort? Here, a monk generates enthusiasm, tries, stirs up energy, takes hold of the mind, and strives for the non-arising of unarisen evil, unbeneficial qualities... for the abandoning of arisen evil, unbeneficial qualities... for the arousing of unarisen beneficial qualities... for the stability, non-decline, increase, maturity, and fulfillment of arisen beneficial qualities. This, monks, is right effort.

---

[3] SN 53
[4] See SN 45.4

14   'And what, monks, is right mindfulness? Here, a monk abides contemplating a body in the body... a feeling in the feelings... a mind in the mind... a dhamma in the dhammas—ardent, clearly comprehending, and mindful, having removed desire and aversion for the world.

15   'And what, monks, is right samādhi? Here, a monk, quite secluded from sensual pleasures, secluded from unbeneficial qualities, enters and abides in the first jhāna, which has initial & sustained application of mind, and rapture & bliss born of seclusion. With the stilling of initial & sustained application of mind, he enters and abides in the second jhāna, where there is inner clarity and unification, without initial & sustained application, but with rapture & bliss born of samādhi. With the fading away of rapture he abides in equanimity, mindful and clearly comprehending, personally experiencing the bliss of which the noble ones say: "Equanimous and mindful, one abides in bliss", he enters and abides in the third jhāna. With the abandoning of bodily pleasure and pain, and the previous ending of mental bliss and suffering, he enters and abides in the fourth jhāna, which is without pleasure and pain, but has mindfulness fully purified by equanimity. This, monks, is right samādhi.'[5]

16   The first factor, right view, includes the knowledge of the path itself. This, to start with, is wisdom in its preliminary role of providing a theoretical understanding of the path as a necessary prerequisite for setting out on the journey. A distorted understanding of the path will surely act as an effective block to successfully arriving at the destination. Indeed, there are many meditators who, starting practice

---

[5]   DN 22.21, MN 141.23–31, SN 45.8

with wrong views, interpret their meditation experiences
so as to confirm and reinforce their misconceptions.[6]

17   But this intellectual understanding is not enough. It must
be accompanied by some feeling for the meaning of suffering, an emotional response to the dilemmas of existence if
it is to provide an effective motivation for action. Hence, the
second path factor is right intention, the emotional counterpart of right view, which enables understanding to mature
into wisdom rather than lapse into cunning. Endowed with
these two, one can rightly undertake the virtues.

18   Right practice of virtue also requires two complementary qualities. Firstly, an understanding of what is right and
wrong together with skill in acting appropriately; secondly,
a feeling of compassion and fear of wrongdoing as motivation. These two qualities will work together in meditation as
samatha and vipassanā until they culminate in the universal
compassion and transcendental wisdom of the arahant.

19   A key benefit of ethical conduct is that it 'leads to samādhi'.[7] Of the basic moral precepts, those on killing and harsh
speech counter the hindrance of ill will, those on stealing
and adultery counter sensual desire, and those on lying and
intoxicants counter delusion. Diligence in executing ones
duties and responsibilities—an important aspect of virtue—
combats sloth & torpor, while sense restraint and contentment further reduce sensual desire. Each facet of virtue
eliminates stress, conflict, and suffering, giving rise to a
quiet ease and confidence of heart. This curbing of gross
defilements lays the groundwork for the more subtle task
of samādhi. So it is that the Buddha declared that purity of

---

[6]   DN 1.1.31*ff.*
[7]   E.g. AN 4.52

virtue and correct view are the 'starting point of beneficial qualities', to be established before undertaking meditation.[8]

20   The last three factors of the path make up the 'aggregate of samādhi'. Right effort, the 'pre-requisite of samādhi', eradicates the hindrance of sloth & torpor. The most interesting of the four right efforts is the last. It points to the importance of not being complacent with whatever good has been achieved. The first task of the meditator who has reached a certain degree of calm is not to rush ahead to insight, but to consolidate samādhi. And remember, 'effort' doesn't mean 'self-torture'.

21   'A lazy person abides in suffering, overwhelmed by evil, unbeneficial qualities, and destroys a great deal of their own good. One with roused up energy abides in bliss, secluded from evil, unbeneficial qualities, and fulfills a great deal of their own good. It is not by the inferior that the topmost is attained; it is by the topmost that the topmost is attained. This holy life, monks, is the cream, and the Teacher is right in front of you. Therefore you should rouse up energy for the attaining of the unattained, for the achieving of the unachieved, for the witnessing of the unwitnessed.'[9]

22   Right mindfulness is defined as the four satipaṭṭhānas. Due to the complexity of the topic, we will treat them under their own section as one of the groups of the Wings to Awakening, rather than under the eightfold path. This is not to hide the crucial fact that satipaṭṭhāna derives its true significance from the fact that they are one of the factors of the path. Since they are included in the 'section on samādhi', rather than the 'section on wisdom', their primary purpose

---

[8]   SN 47.3
[9]   SN 12.22

is to lead to the attainment of jhāna, as the final factor of the path: right samādhi.

Right Samādhi

23   'On the occasion when a noble disciple intends to go forth from the home life into homelessness, he is like the celestial coral tree of the Tāvatimsa deities when the leaves turn brown.

24   'On the occasion when the noble disciple shaves off hair and beard, puts on the dyed robe and goes forth from the home life into homelessness, he is like the celestial coral tree... when the leaves fall.

25   'On the occasion when the noble disciple... enters and abides in the first jhāna, he is like the celestial coral tree... when it is budding.

26   'On the occasion when the noble disciple... enters and abides in the second jhāna, he is like the celestial coral tree... when the shoots appear.

27   'On the occasion when the noble disciple... enters and abides in the third jhāna, he is like the celestial coral tree... when the blossoms form.

28   'On the occasion when the noble disciple... enters and abides in the fourth jhāna, he is like the celestial coral tree... when the flowers are like the red lotus.

29   'On the occasion when the noble disciple, due to the evaporation of the poisons, enters and abides in the poison-free release of heart, release by wisdom, having witnessed it with his own direct knowledge, he is like the celestial coral tree of the Tāvatimsa deities when it is in full bloom.

30   'On that occasion the earth deities proclaim the news: "The venerable one of such & such a name, the student of such & such a venerable one, who went forth from such & such a village or town, has witnessed... the evaporation of the poisons!"... And right at that mo-

ment, that instant, the news soars up [through the various orders of deities] as far as the Brahmā realm. Such is the majesty of one who has evaporated the poisons.'[10]

31   Right samādhi brings together the other seven path factors, issuing in right knowledge and release.

32   'How well described by the Blessed One who knows and sees, the arahant, the fully enlightened Buddha are the seven pre-requisites of samādhi for the development and fulfillment of right samādhi. What seven? Right view, right intention, right speech, right action, right livelihood, right effort, and right mindfulness. One-pointedness of mind with these seven factors as pre-requisites is called noble right samādhi with its vital conditions and with its requisites.'[11]

33   I take 'one-pointedness of mind' in the context of jhāna to imply singleness both of consciousness and of object. That is, jhāna occurs based on mind-consciousness only, without the diversity of sense consciousness; and this mind-consciousness knows just one thing.

34   The word 'point' is a translation of the Pali *agga* (= 'acme'), which has superlative connotations difficult to capture in translation. It should not be taken to imply that jhānas are a cramped, narrow state of mind; rather, they are regularly described as 'vast, exalted, measureless'.

35   It is often asked whether all activity of the five external senses must cease in jhāna. From the evidence of the suttas, this certainly seems to be the case. The jhāna formula begins with 'quite secluded from sensual pleasures'. *Kāma* can, in a typical Pali idiom, refer to either the inner attraction to the

---

[10]   AN 7.65
[11]   DN 18.27; cp. SN 45.28, AN 7.42, MN 117.3

senses, or to the sense objects themselves. Here, the following phrase 'secluded from unbeneficial qualities' obviously includes sensual desire, so 'secluded from sensual pleasures' should refer to, or at least include, the sense objects. In fact, when used in plural form, as here, the term *kāma* normally means the objects of the sense; when speaking of desire for the objects, the singular is used.

36   The suttas regularly contrast the plurality of sense experience with the unity of jhāna, and so the Buddha said that: 'Noise is a thorn to the first jhāna.'[12] This might be understood as saying that 'When sound arises inside the first jhāna it's an obstruction.' However, this is not how it should be read, as is made clear by comparing with the statements which follow: 'Initial & sustained application of mind are a thorn to the second jhāna. Rapture is a thorn to the third jhāna' and so on. Initial & sustained application of mind are incompatible with the second jhāna, cannot exist in it, and if they arise they signify that one has fallen away from second jhāna. So too, sound—and by extension the other sense objects—are incompatible with the first jhāna, cannot exist in it, and if they arise they signify that one has fallen away from first jhāna.

37   The following passage bears on this question.

38   And then Venerable Mahā Moggallāna addressed the monks: 'Here, friends, when I had attained imperturbable samādhi on the bank of the Sappinikā River, I heard the sound of elephants plunging in, crossing over, and trumpeting.' [On which the Buddha commented:] 'The meaning is that that samādhi was not fully purified. Moggallāna spoke truthfully.'[13]

---

[12]   AN 10.72
[13]   Vin Pj 4

39   This episode presumably refers to Venerable Mahā Moggallāna's brief but troubled period of striving for enlightenment. 'Imperturbable' usually means at least fourth jhāna, or, as we have seen earlier, occasionally the formless attainments.[14] Mahā Moggallāna is describing an unusual situation, one striking enough to deserve a special mention. If hearing sounds in samādhi were normal, no explanation would be required. Clearly, the monks doubted Mahā Moggallāna's meaning, and so the Buddha responded by confirming that the samādhi was not perfected, which is why he could still hear sounds.

40   The four jhānas are the ultimate manifestation of the psychology of bliss. The first jhāna occurs with the ending of the five external senses and the five hindrances. Relieved of these burdens, the mind is buoyant and at ease, solely preoccupied with one object, the subtle reflection of the mind derived from the basic meditation subject. Because of the nearness of sense activity and defilement, however, the mind must still actively apply itself to that object, first placing then pressing. This pressing causes the object to recede slightly, so the mind must be re-placed, and so on in an automatic process which causes a slight ripple or wavering in awareness. As the mind gains more inner confidence it no longer needs to apply itself, but can simply be at one with the object. The pulsing effect fades away, leaving the clear stillness characteristic of the second jhāna. The third jhāna is marked by a maturing of the emotional response to blissful feeling. The refined thrill of rapture deepens into

---

[14] The term 'imperturbable' renders the Pali *aneñja*, which appears as part of the stock phrase describing the mind that has developed the fourth jhāna as a basis for higher knowledges: *evaṁ samāhite citte parisuddhe pariyodāte anaṅgaṇe vigatūpakkilese mudubhūte kammaniye ṭhite āneñjappatte...*

the impartial watchfulness of equanimity. Mindfulness and clear comprehension, though like equanimity present from the first jhāna, come to the fore as one is fully immersed in bliss without being elated by it. But even that purified bliss exerts the softest of pulls and must be let go as the mind settles down into the fourth jhāna—pure bright watchfulness. Equanimity is now present as both affective tone and emotional attitude, allowing mindfulness to reach its maximum clarity and power.

41   The relative stability of the four jhānas can be gauged from the length of the rebirth they generate. From practicing the first jhāna, you get reborn in the Brahmā realm for one æon; for second jhāna—two æons; third jhāna—four æons; and fourth jhāna ensures a rebirth of a full five hundred æons.[15] It is the stability of the neutral feeling in fourth jhāna that gives it such potency. It should go without saying that the role of jhāna in Buddhist practice is not to attain such states; but this scale helps reflect on the scale of the jhānas. It would seem that the same power that gives rise to such a long rebirth, for those seeking such a thing, will also be the power that leads to the deepest insights; and the fourth jhāna in particular is normally used as the basis for realization.

42   Right samādhi is further described as having five factors: 'suffusion with rapture, suffusion with bliss, suffusion with heart, suffusion with light, it is the basis of reviewing.'[16] Notice the embodied, 'immanent' language that the Buddha used so typically in describing samādhi. The final of these factors, 'basis of reviewing' is samādhi as a basis for the in-

---

[15] AN 4.123. An æon in Buddhist (or more broadly Indian) cosmology is comparable to the period from one Big Bang to the next.

[16] DN 34.1.6; cp. AN 5.28, DN 2.81

vestigative reviewing knowledge developed upon emerging from jhāna, as described in the following passage.

43   'Just as if, monks, one should review another, or one standing should review one sitting, or one sitting should review one lying down, in the same way a monk has the basis of reviewing well apprehended, well attended, well borne in mind, well penetrated with understanding.'[17]

44   The modern vipassanā schools like to say that jhāna is a pre-Buddhist practice, and hence is suspect, not 'really' Buddhist like vipassanā. However, while there was no doubt some practice of samādhi among preBuddhist ascetics, this was not the same as the Buddhist samādhi. The brahman student Subha said that:

45   'I do not see such a fulfilled noble aggregate of samādhi outside of Buddhism amongst other contemplatives and brahmans.'[18]

46   How is Buddhist samādhi different? I think it's because it is 'noble right samādhi with its pre-requisites', namely, the previous seven factors of the path, starting with right view. The actual state of concentration may be similar, but it plays a different role in the spiritual path.

47   It is associated with five knowledges:

48   'Monks, develop samādhi that is measureless, masterly, and mindful. When samādhi is developed that is measureless, masterly, and mindful, five personal knowledges arise. What five? The personal knowledge arises: "This samādhi is blissful now and results in bliss in the future." ... "This samādhi is noble and spiritual." ... "This samādhi is not cultivated by bad men."

---

[17] AN 5.28
[18] DN 10.2; cp. SN 45.14

... "This samādhi is peaceful and refined, tranquil, unified, not actively controlled or constrained." ... "I enter and emerge mindfully from this samādhi." [19]

49   These descriptions have nothing to do with the concepts of 'momentary samādhi' or transcendental 'path-moment' samādhi. They simply refer to the practice of jhāna by one developing the noble path.

50   The conception of the path as support for noble right samādhi might be described in this way. The course of meditation for one on the noble path has been smoothed by the right view that has eliminated or lessened certain defilements, such as doubt or sensual desire, according to the stage of progress. Furthermore, at the actual time of developing samādhi, the previously developed right view manifests as a clear awareness of what is beneficial and what is unbeneficial, as well as an understanding of the causal relationships between mental factors leading to peace of mind. The path factor of right intention manifests as undistracted application to the meditation object, while the previously purified virtue gives rise to the gladness of non-remorse. Together with energy and mindfulness, these factors lead to jhāna. These jhānas as noble right samādhi itself are similar in their basic functions and natures to jhāna practiced outside the eightfold path. However, due to the exceptional purity of the factors instrumental in their attaining, they are singularly pellucid and tranquil, yielding an intuitive flowering of wisdom. Upon emerging mindfully, the noble one will review the jhāna with wisdom. They will see that the bliss in that jhāna arose from letting go, and that continuing that process of letting go will culminate in the ultimate bliss of Nibbana.

---

[19]   DN 34: 1.6, AN 5.27

51   Noble right samādhi closes the circle: although the last factor of the path, its fruit is the perfection of the first factor, the right view normally associated with the stream-enterer. The path includes the truths, the truths include the path. The Dhamma is like a hologram image: when it is broken, each fragment contains not a part, but the whole of the original image.

52   'Monks, develop samādhi. A monk who has samā-dhi understands in accordance with reality. What does he understand in accordance with reality? He under-stands: This is suffering; this is the origin of suffering; this is the cessation of suffering; this is the way of practice leading to the cessation of suffering.'[20]

The Four Satipaṭṭhānas

53   Right mindfulness, the 'basis of samādhi',[21] is the gate-keeper who lets both samatha and vipassanā enter with their message in accordance with reality. Here, *nimitta*, ren-dered as 'basis', may also mean 'sign', since samādhi is cer-tainly characterized by unobstructed mindfulness; but the intended contextual meaning seems to be that satipaṭṭhāna is a crucial support for samādhi. In keeping with the theme of this essay, of the mutual harmony between all aspects of the path, let us looking more closely at the relationship of mindfulness with samatha and vipassanā.

54   In the analysis that follows, I will not be extensively quot-ing from the Satipaṭṭhāna Sutta as such. This is already widely known and widely available, and if you have not

---

[20]   SN 56.1
[21]   MN 44.12. See Appendix A.

yet read it, you should. My aim is not to explain the Sati-paṭṭhāna Sutta, but to show its deep and rich integration with the very many other teachings on practice found in the texts.

55   Mindfulness may be characterized as the quality of mind that recollects and focuses awareness within an appropriate frame of reference, bearing in mind the what, why, and how of the task at hand. Mindfulness as a mental quality plays a crucial role in recollecting the teachings and applying them to the present moment, thus supporting right view. By re-minding one of what is right and wrong, it supports the sense of conscience which is vital for virtue.

56   Satipaṭṭhāna, the 'establishings of mindfulness', refers to a specific and detailed set of contemplative exercises in which mindfulness plays a prominent role. The 'develop-ment of satipaṭṭhāna' refers to the advanced employment of the basic exercises for the contemplation of imperma-nence. The 'way of practice leading to the development of satipaṭṭhāna' is the noble eightfold path.[22] In this analysis, 'satipaṭṭhāna' seems to have the function of supporting samā-dhi, the 'development of satipaṭṭhāna' that of supporting insight, while both of these in the overall context of the path lead to liberation.

57   The classic formula uses a reflexive idiom, saying one con-templates 'a body in the body'. This is explained in the suttas as: 'the in-and-out breaths are a certain body [among the bodies].'[23] This implies focusing on a specific aspect of the overall framework. The explanation that the phrase means 'contemplating the body as a body (and not as a self or soul)'

[22]   SN 47.40
[23]   MN 118; bracketed phrase omitted at SN 54.10, 13, 16.

does not ring true since the phrase pertains as much to samā-dhi as to insight.

Satipaṭṭhāna and the Hindrances

58   Each of the contemplations in satipaṭṭhāna is qualified by a set of four terms. The first term, 'ardent' refers to energy; the second, 'clearly comprehending' to understanding; the third is mindfulness itself.

59   The fourth term indicates the abandoning of desire and aversion, which are the chief of the five hindrances.[24] The phrase is not further defined here, but the following verses may be relevant. Bearing in mind that sequence in such verses is often quite loose, we may note that these verses follow teachings chiefly on virtue, including sense restraint, but jhāna and samādhi have also been mentioned.

60   'And then there are these five stains in the world
        For the removal of which the mindful one should train.
    One should overcome lust for visible forms
        Sounds, tastes, smells, and touches.

61   'Having removed desire for these phenomena,
        A monk, mindful, with mind well released
    Rightly examining Dhamma at the right time
        Unified, he shatters the darkness.'[25]

62   A series of four 'steps of the Dhamma' lists freedom from desire, freedom from ill will, right mindfulness, and right samādhi. It seems that the preliminary subduing of these hindrances through sense restraint, etc., prepares the mind for mindfulness practice, which is the foundation for the complete eradication of hindrances by right samādhi.

---

[24] *Domanassa* = ill will at Snp 1106 = AN 3.32.
[25] Snp 974, 975

63   'One should abide without desire
       With heart free from ill will
       Mindful, one should be of one-pointed mind
       Well concentrated in samādhi within.'[26]

64   Contemplation of the hindrances present in the mind is part of the preliminary development of satipaṭṭhāna. But during the course of practice they must be fully abandoned if one is to realize any 'truly noble distinctions of knowledge & vision beyond human principles', which include jhāna, psychic powers, the stages of enlightenment, and satipaṭṭhāna itself as a factor of the noble path.[27]

65   'Monks, these five hindrances choke the mind, robbing understanding of its strength. What five?

66   'Sensual desire; ill will; sloth & torpor; restlessness & remorse; and doubt are obstructions and hindrances.

67   'Certainly, monks, that any monk with understanding thus feeble and robbed of strength, not having abandoned these five hindrances that choke the mind, robbing understanding of its strength, would know his own welfare, another's welfare, or the welfare of both, or witness any truly noble distinction of knowledge & vision beyond human principles: that is not possible.

68   'But certainly, monks, that any monk with powerful understanding, having abandoned these five hindrances that choke the mind, robbing understanding of its strength, would know his own welfare, another's welfare, or the welfare of both, or witness any truly noble distinction of knowledge & vision beyond human principles: that is possible.'[28]

---

[26] AN 4.29; cp. AN 4.30

[27] Vin Pj 4.4

[28] AN 5.51

69 It is a common idiom in Pali that the same thing can be spoken of in positive or negative terms, as an attainment or an abandoning. For example, the process of enlightenment can be described either as the successive abandoning of the defilements of self-view, doubt, etc., or as the attaining of the stages of stream-entry, once-return, non-return, and arahant. What then is the positive counterpart of the abandoning of the hindrances?

70 'The first jhāna, friend, abandons five factors and possesses five factors. Here, friend, when a monk has entered upon the first jhāna, sensual desire, ill will, sloth & torpor, restlessness & remorse, and doubt are abandoned. Initial & sustained application of mind, rapture, bliss, and one-pointedness of mind are occurring.'[29]

71 The opposition between jhāna and the five hindrances is not a one-off or occasional teaching, but is a central doctrine, frequently reiterated. It is even enshrined in the basic cosmology of Buddhism, which sees the worlds of rebirth as corresponding to the level of development of mind. One still bound by sensual desire will be reborn in the sensual realm (*kāmaloka*), while one who attains jhāna will be reborn in the Brahma realm. There is no 'access' realm.

72 'What should be done, Anuruddha, by a clansman who has gone forth thus? While he still does not achieve the rapture & bliss that are secluded from sensual pleasures, secluded from unbeneficial qualities, or to something more peaceful than that, desire invades his mind and remains, ill will... sloth & torpor... restlessness & remorse... doubt... cynicism...listlessness invades his mind and remains. When he achieves that rapture & bliss... or something more peaceful than that, desire

---

[29] MN 43.20

does not invade his mind and remain, ill will... sloth &
torpor... restlessness & remorse... doubt... cynicism...
listlessness does not invade his mind and remain.'[30]

73   The following statement by Venerable Ānanda clarifies
the standard the Buddha took for what he considered praise-
worthy meditation, able to go beyond the hindrances.

74   'What kind of jhāna did the Blessed One not praise?
Here, someone abides with a heart dominated by and
prey to lust for sensual pleasures... ill will... sloth & torpor... restlessness & remorse... doubt. Harboring these
qualities within, and not understanding the escape
from these qualities in accordance with reality, they
do jhāna, re-do jhāna, out-do jhāna, and mis-do jhāna.
The Blessed One did not praise this kind of jhāna.

75   'But what kind of jhāna did the Blessed One praise?
Here, a monk... enters and abides in the first jhāna...
second jhāna... third jhāna... fourth jhāna. The Blessed
One praised this kind of jhāna.'[31]

76   Even the transcendental wisdom of the noble ones is unable to suppress the hindrances without the support of jhāna.

77   'Even though a noble disciple has seen clearly with
right understanding in accordance with reality how
sensual pleasures provide little gratification, much
suffering, much despair, with great danger, as long as
he does not attain the rapture & bliss that are apart
from sensual pleasures, apart from unbeneficial qualities, he is not uninvolved in sensual pleasures... But
when he does attain that rapture & bliss... he is uninvolved in sensual pleasures.'[32]

---

[30] MN 68.6
[31] MN 108.26–27
[32] MN 14.4; cp. MN 68.6

78   This passage is one of those that has been used regularly to suggest that jhānas are not really necessary. Using the kind of logic that seems so persuasive to the vipassanā schools, a passage that is taught in order to quite explicitly praise jhāna and emphasize its necessity is pressed into service to argue that a noble disciple need not have jhāna. But the context in no way supports this. The sutta was taught by the Buddha to Mahānāma, a Sakyan layman. His problem is not, 'What is the way of practice to become a stream-enterer?' but 'Now that I am a stream-enterer, how do I deal with sensual desires that arise from time to time?' The Buddha reminds him that, since our pleasure seeking tendencies are so strong, only through the bliss of jhāna are we able to truly let go of the pleasures of the sense. It is Mahānāma's practice, now, that is the issue, not the practice that brought him to stream-entry in the first place. No doubt he could have have attained a peaceful and profound meditation state that lead to his insight, but, like most of us, found it difficult to maintain this in everyday life. His state of realization, of course, would not decay, but as long as he is not fully enlightened defilements can arise from time to time that would obstruct his further progress.

79   The Buddha compared jhāna to gold. As long as the impurities have not been completely removed, gold is not soft, workable, or radiant.

80   'So too, there are these five taints of the mind, tainted by which the mind is not soft, nor workable, nor radiant, but is brittle, and does not have right samādhi for the evaporation of the poisons. What five? Sensual desire, ill will, sloth & torpor, restlessness & remorse, and doubt... But when the mind is released from these five taints, that mind is soft, workable, radiant, not

brittle, it has right samādhi for the evaporation of the poisons.'[33]

81   The phrase 'having removed desire and aversion for the world', found so commonly in the satipaṭṭhāna formula, may be replaced by 'samādhi'.

82   'Monks, those monks who are new, not long gone forth, recently come to this Dhamma and vinaya should be spurred on, encouraged, and established by you in the development of the four establishings of mindfulness. What four? "Come friends, abide contemplating a body in the body... a feeling in the feelings... a mind in the mind... a dhamma in the dhammas—ardent, clearly comprehending, unified, with clarity of mind, concentrated in samādhi, with mind one-pointed for the knowledge of the body... feelings... mind... dhammas in accordance with reality."

83   'Those monks who are trainees, not yet attained to their heart's goal, who abide longing for the unexcelled security from bondage, they too abide contemplating a body in the body... a feeling in the feelings... a mind in the mind... a dhamma in the dhammas [in the same way] for the full knowledge of these things.

84   'Those monks who are arahants, they too abide contemplating a body in the body... a feeling in the feelings... a mind in the mind... a dhamma in the dhammas [in the same way] but detached from these things.'[34]

85   Such passages show that satipaṭṭhāna, far from being separate from or opposed to samatha, is in fact indistinguishable from it. Note that the above passage, as is typical, distinguishes between individuals at various stages of development in terms of the goal, not the mode, of practice. There

---

[33] AN 5.13
[34] SN 47.4

is no suggestion that one in a preliminary stage of development need not develop jhāna, and that this is only necessary for higher attainments. On the contrary, the investigative aspect of satipaṭṭhāna must be balanced with the emotional qualities of joy and serenity if obstacles are to be overcome and insight is to be deepened. This process can proceed in various modes.

86   'Therefore, monk, you should train yourself thus: "My mind will be still and steady within myself, and arisen evil, unbeneficial qualities will not invade my mind and remain."

87   'When this is accomplished, you should train yourself thus: "I will develop the heart's release through loving-kindness... compassion... admiration... equanimity."

88   'When this samādhi is thus developed and made much of, then you should develop this samādhi with initial & sustained application of mind; without initial but with sustained application of mind; with neither initial nor sustained application of mind; with rapture; without rapture; with enjoyment; with equanimity...

89   'When this samādhi is thus developed, well developed, then you should train yourself thus: "I will abide contemplating a body in the body—ardent, clearly comprehending, and mindful, having removed desire and aversion for the world."

90   'When this samādhi is thus developed and made much of, then you should develop this samādhi with initial & sustained application of mind; without initial but with sustained application of mind; with neither initial nor sustained application of mind; with rapture; without rapture; with enjoyment; with equanimity... [And so on for feelings, mind, and dhammas].'[35]

---

[35] AN 8.63

91   Here, satipaṭṭhāna is treated simply as jhāna. This probably refers to jhāna developed using one of the exercises
included in the four satipaṭṭhānas. If one's original mode of
satipaṭṭhāna fails to lead to samādhi, the meditator should
find some way to uplift the mind.

92   'Thus dwelling contemplating a body in the body
[feelings, mind, dhammas], bodily disturbance arises
based on the body [feelings, mind, dhammas], or the
heart is lazy, or the mind is distracted externally. That
monk should direct his mind to some inspiring basis.
Doing so, gladness is born in him. In one who is glad,
rapture is born. In one with rapturous mind, the body
becomes tranquil. One with tranquil body feels bliss.
In one who is blissful, the mind enters samādhi. He
considers thus: "I have accomplished that purpose for
which I directed my mind; now let me withdraw." He
withdraws, and neither initiates nor sustains application of mind. He understands: "I am without initial
& sustained application of mind, I am mindful and
blissful within myself." '[36]

93   Here is another passage, where instead of the phrase 'having removed desire and aversion for the world', the sutta
simply says 'I am blissful'.

94   'He understands: "As I abide contemplating a body
in the body... a feeling in the feelings... a mind in the
mind... a dhamma in the dhammas—ardent, clearly
comprehending, and mindful, I am blissful." '[37]

---

[36] SN 47.10
[37] SN 47.10

The Four Focuses. 1: Body

95 The contemplation of the body begins with mindfulness of breathing. This is therefore the most fundamental satipaṭṭhāna practice. If this is borne in mind, the intimacy between satipaṭṭhāna and samādhi as evidenced in the above passages becomes easily understood.

96 'When mindfulness of breathing is developed and cultivated, it fulfills the four establishings of mindfulness. When the four establishings of mindfulness are developed and cultivated, they fulfill the seven enlightenment factors. When the seven enlightenment factors are developed and cultivated, they fulfill realization and release.'[38]

97 Body contemplation then continues with development of awareness of the body postures, parts of the body, elements, and corpses. The contemplation on parts of the body and corpses is primarily a samatha practice designed to remove lust, and so such a meditator is said to 'not neglect jhāna'.[39]

98 Contemplation of body postures throughout daily activities is a bit of an odd one out here. Such a practice seems insufficient to induce jhāna, and so the appearance of the practice here is a cornerstone of the modern idea that observation of body postures may even replace concentrative meditation. In fact this practice is one of the preliminaries to developing meditation, rather than as meditative practice itself, as is borne out by its constant appearance in the Gradual Training *before* satipaṭṭhāna. Only in this one isolated

---

[38] MN 118.15

[39] AN 1:20. Although I refer to this chapter a few times, it is a highly schematic passage, probably assembled quite late, and in part incongruous. For example, one who develops right speech is said to 'not neglect jhāna', which does not make much sense even if we interpret jhāna here as broadly as 'meditation.'

instance (repeated in the Kāyagatasati Sutta) is this practice treated as if it were part of meditation itself. Most of the non-Pali versions of the Satipaṭṭhāna Sutta in fact omit this practice or place it prior to breath meditation. Nevertheless, it is undeniably true that continuity of mindfulness through the day is crucial to both samatha and vipassanā. As the words 'again and beyond' at the start of each section of the Satipaṭṭhāna Sutta indicate, each exercise contributes a part of the overall meditative development.

99   The Kāyagatasati Sutta repeats each of these contemplations, but brings out the samatha side, saying in each case:

100   'As he abides thus diligent, ardent, and resolute, his memories and intentions based on the household life are abandoned. With their abandoning, his mind becomes steadied within himself, settled, unified, and concentrated in samādhi. That is how a monk develops mindfulness of the body.'[40]

101   The basic purpose of the contemplations on the body parts, elements, and corpses is to rise above sensuality. If one believes that sensuality is an intrinsic quality of human nature, this objective will seem perverse, an unnatural repression leading inevitably to neurosis. Lust can indeed lead to neurosis if it is unacknowledged and denied. But seeing sensual desire, not as a permanent property, but as a conditioned phenomenon, one is free to investigate its effect on the happiness of the mind.

102   Sensual lust is fueled by focusing on the attractiveness of the body. By going against the stream of habit, focusing attention on the unattractive aspect of the body, sensual lust can be seen in sharp relief. This is not repression; quite the

---

[40] MN 119.4*ff.*

opposite, it is broadening our experience to accept unpleasant aspects of our humanity which we normally prefer to repress. When the flame of desire is deprived of its fuel it simply goes out, and the mind experiences a coolness and bliss. Then one knows that the real repression, the real perversion, the real neurosis is the addiction to sensual gratification, locked in place by denying the futility of sense pleasures.

103 But these contemplations do not only bestow the emotional maturity, dignity, and independence that come with freedom from addiction. Being based on inquiry into reality, they also serve to deepen wisdom. The most suggestive description of the contemplation of the parts of the body treats this as a stepping-stone to understanding the consciousness which does not die with the body.

104 'There are, Bhante, these four attainments of vision. Here, a certain contemplative or brahman by means of ardor, striving, devotion, heedfulness, and right attention contacts such a form of heart-samādhi that when his mind is in samādhi he reviews this very body, up from the soles of the feet and down from the tips of the hair, surrounded by skin and full of many kinds of impurities thus: "In this body there are head hairs, body hairs, nails, teeth, skin, flesh, sinews, bones, bone marrow, kidneys, heart, liver, diaphragm, spleen, lungs, large intestines, small intestines, contents of the stomach, feces, bile, phlegm, pus, blood, sweat, fat, tears, grease, spittle, snot, oil of the joints, and urine." This is the first attainment of vision.

105 'Again, having done this and gone beyond it, he reviews a person's skin, flesh, blood, and bones. This is the second attainment of vision.

106 'Again, having done this and gone beyond it, he understands a person's stream of consciousness unbro-

ken on both sides, fixated in this world and in the world beyond. This is the third attainment of vision.
107   'Again, having done this and gone beyond it, he understands a person's stream of consciousness, unbroken on both sides, fixated neither in this world nor in the world beyond. This is the fourth attainment of vision.'[41]

108   The opening phrase is unusual, but occurs again later in the same sutta and also in the Brahmājala Sutta;[42] in both places 'heart-samādhi' definitely means jhāna. The third attainment is the realization of the passing on of consciousness according to dependent origination, which is the realization of the stream-enterer. The fourth attainment describes the arahant. Hence this passage shows that, when used as a basis for samādhi and insight, body contemplation is not merely a way to get beyond desire, but leads to emancipation from suffering.

109   In the following passage, the contemplation of the four elements forms a part of the practice directed towards the 'imperturbable', which as we have remarked, normally refers to fourth jhāna.

110   'Again, monks, a noble disciple reflects thus: "There are sensual pleasures here & now and sensual pleasures in lives to come. Whatever physical form there is, is the four great elements and physical form derived from the four great elements." Practicing in this way and frequently abiding thus, his mind becomes clear about this base. When there is full clarity he attains to the imperturbable now or he decides upon understanding. With the breaking up of the body, after death,

---

[41] DN 28.7
[42] DN 1.1.31

> it is possible that his on-flowing consciousness will
> pass on to the imperturbable.'[43]

111   Notice the order of the teaching: sensuality; body contemplation; jhāna; understanding rebirth. It would seem that it is no coincidence that descriptions of 'near-death experiences' so uncannily resemble the experience of jhāna. We will return again to the intimate connection between the mind in jhāna set free from the body and the understanding of the process of rebirth.

The Four Focuses. 2: Feelings

112   Normally in Buddhism, 'feeling' (*vedanā*) simply refers to the hedonic or affective tone of experience. The Satipaṭṭhāna Sutta describes the contemplation of feelings as the understanding of pleasant, painful, and neutral feelings, both carnal and spiritual. However, the equivalent section of the Ānāpānasati Sutta brings in rapture—the emotional response to pleasant feeling—and mental activities (*cittasaṅkhārā*), which are defined in the context of mindfulness of breathing as feeling and perception.[44] This seems to broaden the scope of feelings here as far as 'emotions', 'moods'.

113   The important thing, however, is that when these 'feelings' are explicitly analyzed in the suttas, they are identified with the feelings experienced in jhāna.

114   'What is carnal rapture? Rapture which arises dependent on the five cords of sensual pleasures. What is spiritual rapture? Here, a monk enters and abides in the first jhāna... second jhāna. What is even more

---

[43] MN 106.4
[44] MN 44.14

> spiritual rapture? Rapture which arises when a monk
> whose poisons are evaporated reviews his mind re-
> leased from lust, anger, and delusion.'[45]

115   Pleasant and neutral feelings are described in similar
terms, except pleasant spiritual feelings apply to the first
three jhānas, while neutral spiritual feelings only exist in
the fourth jhāna. This analysis of feelings is specific to the
Satipaṭṭhāna Sutta, and the suttas do not offer any alter-
nate explanation. Occasionally, it is true, 'spiritual rapture'
is used prior to jhāna, but this is not part of the full set of
contemplations as found in the Satipaṭṭhāna Sutta; moreover, in such contexts it appears as one of the conditions
leading to full samādhi, not a replacement for it.[46] Reading
straightforwardly from the suttas, contemplation of feelings
in satipaṭṭhāna requires the experience of jhāna.

116   The last of these contemplation is the arahant's 'reviewing knowledge'. This is specifically distinguished from the
feelings in the jhānas, and hence one cannot argue that this
can replace jhāna.[47]

The Four Focuses. 3: Mind

117   'Mind' (*citta*), in Pali as in English, can convey a wide
variety of connotations. Here, as will be clarified below, it
means specifically 'cognition', that is, the faculty of awareness itself, as distinct from associated factors such as feeling,

---

[45] SN 36.31; cp. Thag 85

[46] E.g. SN 46.3 quoted below

[47] These 'even more spiritual feelings' seem to be similar to the 'feelings
based on renunciation' mentioned elsewhere, which however, since
they follow on 'seeing with right understanding in accordance with
reality', seem broader, pertaining to stream-entry and beyond. See
MN 137.11, 15

emotion, thought, volition, etc. This inner sense of knowing receives the information conveyed through the senses,
supplemented and processed by these associated factors.

118   As the 'lord of the city seated at the crossroads' it is the
core of experience; but like any ruler it can maintain its
position only with the help of its auxiliaries. The quality
of the information received is the critical determinant of
the quality of awareness. Also like any ruler, it often seems
that the auxiliaries impede rather than facilitate the flow of
information. The more we try to see the 'boss', the more we
are sidetracked with some underling.

119   The preliminary stages of this section involve contemplating the mind as colored by the presence or absence of greed,
anger, and delusion. These accompanying factors are crude
and domineering, and the contemplation necessarily coarse
and incomplete. In the later stages the mind is contemplated
in its pure form, as 'exalted', 'unexcelled', 'concentrated', 'released'—all terms for jhāna.

120   Just as the contemplation of feelings culminates with the
supreme equanimity of the fourth jhāna, here too the term
'unexcelled' implies the 'unexcelled purity of mindfulness
and equanimity' of the fourth jhāna.[48]

121   This contemplation of mind, with its implicit distinction
between the mind and the defilements which soil it, evokes
the famous—and famously misquoted—statement about
the radiant mind. The words 'original mind' or 'naturally
radiant' do not occur here or elsewhere in the suttas. The
'radiant mind' is a term for jhāna.[49] Here, 'development of
the mind' seems to be a synonym for 'noble right samādhi'.
The significance of the radiant mind is simply this—when

---

[48] MN 54.22-24, MN 53.20-22
[49] SN 46.33, AN 5.23

the lights are on, a clear-sighted person can see what is there.

122   'Monks, this mind is radiant, but tainted by tran-
          sient taints. An unlearned ordinary person does not
          understand this in accordance with reality. That is why
          I say there is no development of the mind for the un-
          learned ordinary person.

123   'Monks, this mind is radiant, and freed from tran-
          sient taints. A learned noble disciple understands this
          in accordance with reality. That is why I say there is
          development of the mind for the learned noble disci-
          ple.'[50]

The Four Focuses. 4: Dhammas

124   What does *dhammas* mean here? *Dhammas* is used in the
Satipaṭṭhāna Sutta in its catch-all role, including *what* is
experienced (phenomena), *how* experience operates (principles), and the meaningful description of experience (teachings). In research subsequent to the original publication of
this work, I concluded that the specification of the contemplation of *dhammas* was originally much narrower, compris-
ing just the five hindrances and the seven awakening factors.
In *A History of Mindfulness* I have argued this point in detail.
For the current work, however, I have chosen to proceed
based on the Pali texts as they are.

125   Contemplation of *dhammas* is often translated as contemplation of 'mental phenomena' or 'mental objects'. The practices detailed in the sutta, however, cover a much a broader
scope than 'mental phenomena'. The contemplation of mental phenomena, not found in the Satipaṭṭhāna Sutta as such,
is a minor practice taught only occasionally: the realization

---

[50] AN 1: 6.1, 2

of feelings, perceptions, and thoughts as they rise, remain, and end.[51] This practice is called a 'development of samādhi'. In teaching sequence it appears after jhāna and before the contemplation of the five aggregates. Its fruit is said to be 'mindfulness & clear comprehension', but it is not said to lead to awakening as such. This is because mental phenomena are the known, not the knowing; insight frees only when the radical impermanence of consciousness itself is brought within its fold.

126   The contemplation of dhammas begins with contemplation of the five hindrances present and absent. The diversity of these hindrances demands a diversity of approaches for their elimination.

127   Sensual desire colors the mind like water dyed vivid blue or crimson, making it attractive but opaque.[52] The most important counter measures are sense restraint and the meditation on ugliness.

128   Ill will is a fire which heats the mind until it is boiling, bubbling, and steaming. It is overcome by loving-kindness. The Buddha said that by using mindfulness alone it is not possible to fully overcome ill will.

129
>   'It is always good for the mindful
>   The mindful one thrives in bliss
>   It is better each day for the mindful one
>   But he is not released from enmity.

---

[51]   DN 33.11 etc
[52]   These similes at AN 3.193.

130   'One whose mind all day and night
  Finds delight in harmlessness
  Who has loving-kindness for all living beings
  For him there is enmity with none.'[53]

131   Sloth & torpor is like a mossy, slimy weed overgrowing the clear waters of the mind. It is overcome by initiative, by putting forth effort, by sustained exertion, by not being complacent; the recommended meditation subject is the perception of light.

132   Restlessness & remorse are like strong winds which lash and stir up the mind into ripples and waves. Restlessness manifests as the inability to stay with one object for a long time. The Buddha was very explicit on how to overcome this:

133   'Samatha should be developed to abandon restlessness.'[54]

134   Or again:

135   'Mindfulness of breathing should be developed to abandon scatteredness of heart.'[55]

136   Remorse (*kukkucca*, literally 'bad-done-ness') is chiefly worry over breaches of virtue, or regret over mistakes made or things left undone in the past. Restlessness runs on to the future; remorse dredges up the past. Their antidote, keeping the mind content in the here & now, is bliss: the pervasive drenching of the whole field of awareness with serene, sublime, sustained ecstasy.

137   Doubt makes the mind turbid, muddy, and dark. It is overcome by 'paying attention to the root'.[56] The 'root' or basis

---

[53] SN 1.813, 814

[54] AN 6.116

[55] AN 6.115

[56] AN 1.2

of meditation is just the meditation object itself. Unwavering continuity of application defines the object, dispelling doubt.

138   It is worth noting that mindfulness is nowhere singled out as being in and of itself capable of overcoming any hindrance. Only when working together with the other factors of jhāna can this occur. The following passage makes this clear. The meditator abandons the hindrances and does satipaṭṭhāna; but the subsequent paragraph shows that this 'satipaṭṭhāna' is in fact the first jhāna. To deepen one's satipaṭṭhāna one must deepen one's practice of jhāna.

139   'Having abandoned these five hindrances, taints of
           the mind which rob understanding of its strength, he
           abides contemplating a body in the body... a feeling in
           the feelings... a mind in the mind... a dhamma in the
           dhammas...

140   'Then the Tathāgata leads him further on: "Come
           monk, abide contemplating a body in the body... a feel-
           ing in the feelings... a mind in the mind... a dhamma
           in the dhammas... but do not apply the mind to these
           things." With the stilling of initial & sustained appli-
           cation of mind, he enters and abides in the second
           jhāna...'[57]

141   After dealing with the hindrances, the next section in the Pali Satipaṭṭhāna Sutta deals with the classic vipassanā exercise of observing the rise and fall of the five aggregates.

142   'Monks, develop samādhi. A monk with samādhi
           understands in accordance with reality. What does
           he understand in accordance with reality? The ori-
           gin and ending of physical form, feeling, perception,
           conceptual activities, and consciousness. What is the

---

[57] MN 125.22–25 condensed

origin of physical form?... For one who relishes, welcomes, and remains attached to physical form, relishing arises. Relishing for physical form is grasping. Due to grasping as condition there is [ongoing] existence. Due to existence as condition, there is birth. Due to birth as condition, aging & death, sorrow, lamentation, bodily pain, mental suffering, and despair come to be. Thus there is the origin of this entire mass of suffering. [And so on for the other four aggregates.]

143   'And what is the ending of physical form?... For one who does not relish, welcome, and remain attached to physical form, relishing for physical form ceases. Due to the cessation of relishing, grasping ceases. Due to the cessation of grasping, [ongoing] existence ceases. Due to the cessation of existence, birth ceases. Due to the cessation of birth, aging & death, sorrow, lamentation, bodily pain, mental suffering, and despair cease. Thus there is the cessation of this entire mass of suffering. [And so on for the other four aggregates.]'[58]

144   Here, understanding impermanence is not the perception of conditioned phenomena arising and passing instantaneously, but understanding how attachment leads to rebirth in accordance with dependent origination. As always, such profound insights arise due to the clarity of the mind in samādhi.

145   The next, closely related, practice is the observation of the six internal and external sense bases, and the fetters that bind these together. Once again, this practice is explicitly said to be dependent on developing samādhi.

146   'Monks, develop samādhi. A monk with samādhi understands in accordance with reality. What does he understand in accordance with reality? He understands: "The eye is impermanent. Visible forms are imperma-

---

[58] SN 22.5

nent. Eye-consciousness is impermanent. Eye contact is impermanent. Feeling arisen due to eye contact... is impermanent. [And so on for the ear, etc.]'[59]

147   The contemplation of dhammas also includes the contemplation of the seven enlightenment factors—mindfulness, investigation of dhammas, energy, rapture, tranquility, samādhi, and equanimity, discussed in more detail below—and their 'fulfillment by development.' Here, samādhi is not merely implied, as it has been in other sections of the Satipaṭṭhāna Sutta, but is mentioned by name, and the satipaṭṭhāna meditator is told to fulfill this samādhi through development.

148   The final section is the contemplation of the four noble truths. Elsewhere, the Buddha said these are taught for 'one who feels':

149   'It is for one who feels that I declare: "This is suffering; this is the origin of suffering; this is the cessation of suffering; this is the way of practice leading to the cessation of suffering."'[60]

150   The point here is that the experience of suffering is fundamental to our spiritual pursuit. Pain is not an incidental to the practice, it underlies it. To understand the four noble truths is not to make oneself experience even more pain, but to understand how to transcend pain through letting go. The bliss of jhāna is a crucial teaching, showing us clearly and directly that suffering arises from our attachments. This is why it is regarded as a foretaste of Nibbana.

151   The four noble truths are briefly mentioned in the Satipaṭṭhāna Sutta (Majjhima Nikāya 10), but are described in detail in the Mahā Satipaṭṭhāna Sutta (Dīgha Nikāya 22).

---

[59] SN 35.99; cp. SN 35.160
[60] AN 3.61

Actually, DN 22 is nothing more than a late expansion of MN 10, with the expanded section on the four noble truths taken from the Saccavibhaga Sutta (MN 141) and inserted by the redactors. It is not an authentic teaching of the Buddha, but nevertheless it gives an idea how these things were understood by the Theravādin redactors, perhaps 200–300 years after the Buddha.[61]

152   The first noble truth is the various kinds of suffering headed by birth, aging, and death; the second is 'that craving which generates repeated existence'; while the third is the ending of that very same craving. The fourth noble truth, the way of practice, is the noble eightfold path as detailed above, including the four jhānas as right samādhi. Thus, once again, the Theravādin scriptures explicitly include jhāna as an integral part of satipaṭṭhāna practice.

Insight

153   Each exercise included in the four establishings of mindfulness concludes with a passage describing various aspects of insight development. This 'insight refrain' is a template for understanding how these practices are meant to be applied in this context.

154   These 'refrain' sections vary considerably between the different versions, and the Pali sutta is one of the few to so strongly emphasize vipassanā here. For example, in the version of this material that is found in the Pali Abhidhamma Vibhaga, there is no mention of a vipassanā refrain.

155   It seems that it is the presence of this refrain, which constantly reinforces the message of vipassanā, which has given rise to the unique modern Theravādin idea that satipaṭṭhāna

---

[61] This is discussed in detail in *A History of Mindfulness*.

is essentially a vipassanā practice. It is crucial to realize that this refrain is an unusual feature of one particular text, and does not represent the teachings on satipaṭṭhāna found elsewhere. In over 70 suttas dealing with satipaṭṭhāna in the Pali canon alone, only two or three others even mention impermanence. Contrast this with the dozens of cases where satipaṭṭhāna is closely associated with samādhi. The modern doctrine of 'satipaṭṭhāna = vipassanā' is an artifact of a selective and misrepresentative reading of the texts.

156   Nevertheless, despite our strong reservations about the authenticity of this passage, and its over-emphasis in modern teachings, we'll still have a look at it and show that, while vipassanā is being emphasized, especially in the section on rise and fall, this is by no means separate from samatha.

Insight 1: Internal and external

157   First, one contemplates 'within oneself' and 'externally.' This phrase is commonly mentioned in the Pali, but is rarely defined explicitly. The following passage is perhaps the only place where we are given a clearer idea of what this contemplation involves in the context of satipaṭṭhāna. As so often, the suttas themselves say that samādhi and satipaṭṭhāna are closely linked.

158   'Here, good man, a monk abides contemplating a body in the body within himself—ardent, clearly comprehending, and mindful, having removed desire and aversion for the world. As he abides thus he becomes concentrated therein with right samādhi, with right clarity. Rightly concentrated and clear therein, he gives rise to knowledge & vision of the bodies of others

externally. [And so on for feelings, mind, and dhammas.]'[62]

159   This explanation shows that the 'internal' contemplation
is the preliminary satipaṭṭhāna meditation that leads to
jhāna. This would normally be one of the objects such as the
breath. The breath is 'internal' to one's own experience of
one's body. Focusing awareness there, the mind is restrained
from wandering 'outside' and becomes peaceful and still 'inside', from the subjective perspective of the meditator. Only
when this process is complete may the meditator then extend their awareness 'outside'.

160   The phrase 'knowledge & vision' refers to the various psychic powers, such as the divine ear or the divine eye, which
enable a meditator who has developed the ultra-refined consciousness of jhāna to extend their awareness of externals.
Since by this stage the mind is very still and the hindrances
are completely absent, there is no danger that the meditator will become distracted or lose focus in this 'external'
contemplation.

Insight 2: Impermanence

161   The second aspect of insight development is the contemplation of the principles of origination and dissolution. Here
is story that exemplifies the the suttas' pragmatic approach
to impermanence.

162   'Long ago, monks, there was a teacher called Araka,
a ford-crosser, free from lust for sensual pleasures,
with many hundreds of disciples. Araka the teacher
taught Dhamma to his disciples thus: "Short is the life
of humans, limited and trifling, with much suffering,

---

[62] DN 18.26

much despair. Wake up by using your mind! Do good! Live the holy life! There is none born who does not die! Just as a drop of dew on the tip of a blade of grass when the sun rises... Just as a bubble in the water appears when it rains... Just as a line drawn on water with a stick... Just as a mountain stream, traveling far, fast flowing, sweeping all before it, never pausing for a moment, a second, an instant, but ever going on, rolling on, surging on... Just as a man might form a gob of spit on the tip of his tongue and spit it out easily... Just like a lump of meat thrown on an iron griddle which has been heated all day... Just like a cow being led to the slaughter, with each step she is closer to being killed, closer to death; in the same way the life of humans is like a cow to be slaughtered, limited and trifling, with much suffering, much despair. Wake up by using your mind! Do good! Live the holy life! There is none born who does not die!"

163 Now at that time, monks, the life span of humans was sixty thousand years, and girls were marriageable at five hundred years. Humans had only six afflictions: cold, heat, hunger, thirst, excrement, and urine. And yet even though humans were of such long life, duration, and little affliction, still Araka the teacher taught Dhamma in that way... But now who lives long lives but a hundred years or a little more... I have done for you what should be done by a teacher seeking the welfare of his disciples out of compassion. Here, monks, are roots of trees, here are empty huts. Practice jhāna, monks! Do not be negligent! Do not regret it later! This is our instruction to you.'[63]

164 This is a fable, a legend of long ago, and it is not so important whether it was meant to be taken literally as it is to

---

[63] AN 7.70

understand the message: all things that we hold on to in life will fall away.

165   I mentioned earlier that the suttas rarely discuss impermanence in the context of satipaṭṭhāna, except for the Satipaṭṭhāna Sutta. Luckily however, in the main case where this does happen, the text gives a clear and explicit explanation. Here is the sutta text.

166   'The body originates due to the origination of nutriment; the body ends due to the cessation of nutriment. Feelings originate due to the origination of contact; feelings end due to the cessation of contact. The mind originates due to the origination of mentality & physical form; the mind ends due to the cessation of mentality & physical form. Dhammas originate due to the origination of attention; dhammas end due to the cessation of attention.'[64]

167   Taken in isolation, this passage probably doesn't make much sense. But each of these terms is well-defined elsewhere in the suttas.

Insight 2.1: Impermanence of the Body

168   The origin of the body is said to be 'nutriment' (āhāra), which here means simply material food. On a basic level, this simply means that food is what sustains the body, with all that implies. We are dependent on the means of producing food, so ensuring that there is bread on the table has been one of humanities most pressing needs, right down to the present day. As long as we are still in this realm, in this 'body built up out of rice and bread', then the search for and reliance on food will never end. So much of our mental

---

[64] SN 47.42

energy revolves around food, the getting, preparing, and eating of it. Small wonder that the Buddha pointed out that attachment to food is one of the forces driving rebirth.

169   'Just as if a painter or an artist with paint or resin of turmeric, blue, or crimson were to create an image of a man or a woman on a well-polished board or a canvas; in just the same way, if there is lust, relishing, and craving for material food, consciousness becomes fixated there and grows. Where consciousness is fixated and growing, there is the reincarnation of mentality & physical form... the growth of conceptual activities... appearance in repeated existence in the future... birth, aging, and death in the future... that is sorrowful, depressing, and full of despair, I say.'[65]

Insight 2.2: Impermanence of Feelings

170   The origin of feelings is said to be 'contact' (perhaps 'stimulus' would be a better rendering of the Pali *phassa*). 'Contact' is the normal condition for feeling in dependent origination (and is also the condition for perception and conceptual activities).[66] Contact is said to be the coming together of three things: the internal sense organ (e.g. 'eye'), the external sense object ('form') and the corresponding consciousness ('visual consciousness'). The following passage beautifully shows how deep insight into the dependence of feeling on contact is related to samādhi. The 'purified equanimity' that the passage speaks of is, of course, the equanimity of the fourth jhāna.

171   [When contemplation of the five material elements is completed:] 'Further, monk, there remains only con-

---

[65] SN 12.64
[66] SN 22.56, SN 22.82, etc.

sciousness, purified and bright. And what does one cognize with that consciousness? One cognizes: "pleasure"—"pain"—"neither pain nor pleasure." Dependent on a contact to be felt as pleasant arises pleasant feeling. Feeling that pleasant feeling, one understands: "I feel a pleasant feeling." One understands: "Due to the cessation of just that contact to be felt as pleasant, the corresponding pleasant feeling... ceases and stills." [And so on for painful and neutral feelings.]

172 'Just as from the contact and friction of two sticks, heat is born, fire appears, and due to the separation and laying down of those same two sticks that corresponding heat ceases and stills...

173 'And further there remains only equanimity, purified and bright, soft, workable, and radiant. Suppose a skilled goldsmith or goldsmith's apprentice were to prepare a furnace and heat the crucible, take some gold in a pair of tongs and place it in the crucible. Then from time to time he would blow air, from time to time he would sprinkle water, and from time to time he would watch over with equanimity. The gold would become refined, well refined, thoroughly refined, cleansed, rid of dross, soft, workable, and radiant, and could be used for whatever kind of adornment be desired, whether bracelets, earrings, necklaces, or golden garlands. So too, there remains only equanimity, purified and bright, soft, workable, and radiant.

174 'He understands thus: "If I were to apply this equanimity so pure and bright to the base of infinite space... the base of infinite consciousness... the base of nothingness... the base of neither perception nor non perception, and develop my mind accordingly, this equanimity of mine, dependent on that, grasping that as its fuel, would endure for a long time..." He understands thus: "That is conditioned [by conceptual activities]."

175   'He does not form any volition or act of will for existence or non-existence... He does not grasp at anything
in the world. Not grasping, he is not anxious. Not being anxious, he personally attains final Nibbana. He
understands: "Birth is destroyed; the holy life has been
lived; what was to be done has been done; there is no
returning to this state of existence."

176   'If he feels a pleasant... painful... neither painful
nor pleasant feeling he understands: "That is impermanent..." "That is not adhered to..." "That is not relished..." He feels it as one detached. Feeling a feeling of
the ending of the body he understands: "I am feeling
a feeling of the ending of the body." Feeling a feeling
of the ending of life he understands: "I am feeling a
feeling of the ending of life." He understands: "With
the breaking up of the body, at the end of life, all that
is felt, not being relished, will become cool right here."

177   'Just as a lamp burning dependent on oil and wick,
with the finishing of that oil and wick, without any
other fuel, would be quenched with no fuel...'[67]

Insight 2.3: Impermanence of the Mind

178   In the discussion of the conditions for the four satipaṭṭhānas, the Buddha said that the condition for the mind is 'mentality & materiality' (*nāmarūpa*). Once more, this definition,
while initially obscure, refers to a well-defined set of concepts used in dependent origination.

179   There is a difference in that in dependent origination
the term *viññāṇa* ('consciousness') is used instead of *citta*
(mind). Actually, here as usual the two words are synonyms.
The difference is not in the meaning of the words, but in
their connotations. *Citta* is frequently used in the context

---

[67] MN 140.19-24

of practice, where it signifies the 'developed mind' of samādhi; while *viññāṇa* is more typically used in an analytical
vipassanā-style context. In other words, *citta* pertains to
the fourth noble truth, while *viññāṇa* pertains to the first
three. In satipaṭṭhāna, we have a context which, although
primarily used for teaching how to develop the *citta* as part
of the fourth noble truth, is here being extended to cover
the understanding of impermanence, and so it is treated in
a way similar to *viññāṇa*.

180   In the context of dependent origination, 'mentality' is
defined as feeling, perception, volition, contact, and attention. 'Physical form' is the elements of earth, water, fire,
and air, as well as derived physical form.[68] Together, these
correspond with the first four of the five aggregates (physical form, feeling, perception, conceptual activities), which
are called the 'stations for consciousness'.[69] In other words,
these factors are the support based on which consciousness
thrives.

181   They support consciousness in a number of ways. Physical form directly supports consciousness as the external
objects of the senses, as well as in the subtle 'forms'—images,
etc.—which, though appearing in mind-consciousness, retain certain physical qualities, such as color and shape. In
addition, physical form makes up the body, which provides
the physical basis for the sense organs.

182   The components of mentality can support consciousness
directly as object—as, for example, when one is aware of
a feeling or memory - or indirectly by performing essen-

---

[68] SN 12.2
[69] SN 22.55 etc. *Nāma* in the suttas excludes consciousness, and so is
not a blanket term for the four mental aggregates, although it is often
used as such in later literature.

tial cognitive functions. For example, feeling provides the affective tone that attracts or repels consciousness; perception provides the framework for making sense of experience, and so on. At a basic level these factors make sense-consciousness work; on more complex levels they weld the diverse elements of experience into the elaborate superstructures of language and concepts. This is why the Pali word we have translated as 'mentality' is *nāma*, literally 'name'.

183   All this is external, or objective, to consciousness, defining, determining, and delimiting subjective experience.

184   The terminology of *nāma-rūpa* was adopted by the Buddha from the pre-Buddhist Upaniṣadic philosophy. In the Upaniṣads, *nāma-rūpa* refers to the limited and diverse 'names' and 'shapes' in the world, each of which has its own identity, like a river; but for the enlightened one they flow and merge together into infinite consciousness, like the great ocean. In stating that consciousness was itself dependent on *nāma-rūpa*, the Buddha was turning this Upaniṣadic idea on its head. Consciousness is not an independent metaphysical absolute, but a part of everyday empirical reality, as fragile and dependent as anything else. Consciousness grows or decays together with *nāma-rūpa* at each stage in a person's life.

185   'If, Ānanda, consciousness were not reincarnated in the mother's womb, would mentality & physical form take shape in the mother's womb?'

186   'No, Bhante.'

187   'If, Ānanda, consciousness having been reincarnated in the mother's womb were to be miscarried, would mentality & physical form appear into this state of existence?'

188   'No, Bhante.'

189   'If, Ānanda, the consciousness of a young boy or girl
        were to be cut off, would mentality & physical form
        attain to growth, increase, and maturity?'

190   'No, Bhante.'...

191   'If, Ānanda, consciousness were not fixated in men-
        tality & physical form, would the production of birth,
        aging, death, and the origin of suffering in the future
        be found?'

192   'No, Bhante.'[70]

193   It is simply the nature of the mind to pass away, but it
        is not content to leave no trace; instead, the inner world of
        the mind becomes amplified through the force of kamma
        into the worlds of rebirth, also called 'stations for conscious-
        ness'.[71]

194   This process depends on the idea of 'self', which is in-
        timately linked with labels and language. We stick a label
        saying 'I, me, mine' on the diverse items of baggage in expe-
        rience, which one then feels obliged to claim and lug around.
        Moment to moment, year to year, life to life, the baggage
        changes but the message on the labels stays the same. The
        construction of a 'self', which takes up so much of our men-
        tal energy, is a device to convince us that 'I' will last forever,
        despite the fact that everything changes. Even death is not
        enough to let go. Thus the fascination of the mind with its
        makings is the thread which weaves the fabric of time.

195   'Thus far, Ānanda, could one be born, age, die, pass
        away, and be reborn; thus far is the range of designa-
        tion; thus far is the range of language; thus far is the
        range of concepts; thus far is the domain of under-
        standing; thus far whirls the round for describing this

---

[70] DN 15.21
[71] DN 15.33

state of existence, that is: mentality & physical form together with consciousness.'[72]

196   The impermanence and mutual dependence of *nāma-rūpa* and consciousness, then, is a very profound thing, perhaps the most profound of the Buddha's insights. It does not mean that one simply observes the rise and fall of the stuff of experience that appears in the present moment. It is about the untying of existence; the ending of time itself.

197   'Just as when ghee or oil is burnt, neither ashes nor soot are to be found, so too when Dabba Mallaputta rose into the air and, seated cross legged in the sky, attained final Nibbana after attaining to and withdrawing from the fire element, his body burnt up and neither ashes nor soot were to be found.'

198   And the Blessed One, realizing the meaning of that, was then inspired to utter:

199   'The body broke up, perception ceased
                   Feelings all disappeared
               Conceptual activities were calmed
                 And consciousness came to an end.'[73]

Insight 2.4: Impermanence of Dhammas

200   Once again, the saying that 'dhammas are originated by attention' might seem obscure, but a little inquiry shows the meaning clearly enough. 'Attention' is the normal rendering of the Pali *manasikāra*. It refers to the act of turning the mind, for example to a sense field or a topic of inquiry. In Buddhist psychology it is closely associated with investigation into causality; so *manasikāra* is normally prefixed by *yoniso*. The *yoni* is the womb, so *yoniso manisikāra* is paying attention to

---

[72]   DN 15.22
[73]   Ud 8.9

the root or cause; the opposite, *ayoniso manasikāra*, means paying attention away from the root; in other words, allowing the mind to drift from what is essential, to wander off the topic and be confused about what is happening.

201   In saying that dhammas are originated by attention, the Buddha is pointing out, in particular, the relation between the five hindrances and the seven enlightenment factors. These two sets of dhammas are frequently set against one another. The meditator is said to give rise to the hindrances by paying 'attention away from the root', while the enlightenment factors are developed by 'paying attention to the root'. This is pointing to the conditioned nature of these mental qualities. Good and bad qualities do not just happen—they have a cause. By understanding that cause, and using the mind in the right way, bad qualities can be undone and good qualities increased.

202   My comparative study of this part of the Satipaṭṭhāna Sutta has convinced me that this is what is what is meant by saying that dhammas are originated by attention, a conclusion supported by the traditional commentary on this phrase. Nevertheless, as it stands today the text has a broader application, since 'paying attention to the root' is fundamental to the investigation of the other categories included in the contemplation of dhammas, such as the five aggregates, the six senses, and especially the four noble truths.

203   'Due to not paying attention to dhammas unfit for
        attention and to paying attention to dhammas fit for
        attention, unarisen poisons do not arise and arisen
        poisons are abandoned. He pays attention to the root:
        "This is suffering"... "This is the origin of suffering"...
        "This is the cessation of suffering"... "This is the way of
        practice leading to the cessation of suffering." Paying
        attention in this way, three fetters are abandoned in

him: identity view, doubt, and misapprehension of
virtue & vows.'[74]

204   By bringing in the investigation into causality so explicitly here, the Buddha is emphasizing the strong role that
wisdom plays in this final of the four satipaṭṭhānas.[75] But
this inquiry is not divorced from the tranquility that has
been so characteristic of the Buddha's whole approach to
meditation. On the contrary, it is understanding how cause
and effect works in the very process of meditation itself, as
is shown in the teaching on the 'nine dhammas that are very
helpful'.

205   'What nine dhammas are very helpful? The nine
dhammas rooted in paying attention to the root. In
one paying attention to the root, gladness is born. In
one who is glad, rapture is born. In one with rapturous
mind, the body becomes tranquil. One with tranquil
body feels bliss. In one who is blissful, the mind enters
samādhi. With mind in samādhi, one knows & sees
in accordance with reality. Knowing & seeing in accordance with reality, one is repulsed. Being repulsed,
lust fades away. Due to fading away, one is released.
These are the nine dhammas that are very helpful.'[76]

206   This passage suggests the meaning of 'paying attention
to the root': a systematic, thoroughgoing inquiry, not distracted by superficial issues, which focuses awareness precisely where it counts, staying at that point until it opens up
to wisdom, and the mind moves not onwards, but inwards;

---

[74] MN 2.10, 11

[75] 'Attention' is prominently featured in the context of dependent origination, e.g. DN 14.2.18. Incidentally, in the phrase appearing below at
DN 14.2.21 'the vipassanā path to enlightenment', the word 'vipassanā'
was inserted into the PTS Pali from the commentary despite lacking
any manuscript support.

[76] DN 34.2.2

not from one leaf to another to another, but from a leaf to a branch to the trunk and all the way down to the roots.

Insight 3: Knowledge

207   The third aspect of insight development involves the establishing of mindfulness only for a measure of knowledge and mindfulness. The kinds of knowledge that can be developed are not described further. The interpretation of the vipassanā schools would bring in the socalled 'insight-knowledges' here. But this list dates from many centuries after the Buddha and cannot have been meant here.

208   Luckily, there is a sutta where Venerable Anuruddha details the kinds of knowledge obtainable by satipaṭṭhāna. Many of these are normally associated with samādhi practice, especially the various kinds of psychic knowledge. But in the suttas they belong firmly in the wisdom category. As with all deep wisdom, the suttas state that these knowledges are 'for one with samādhi, not for one without samādhi.'[77]

209   'It is from the development and making much of these four establishings of mindfulness that I have attained such great direct knowledge... I directly know a thousand worlds...' 'I recollect a thousand æons...' 'I wield the various kinds of psychic powers...' 'I have the purified divine ear, which surpasses the human...' 'I understand the minds of other beings...' 'I understand in accordance with reality the possible as possible, and the impossible as impossible...' 'I understand in accordance with reality the fruits of undertaking actions past, future, and present...' '...the goals of all paths of practice...' '...the many and various elements...' '...the various dispositions of beings...' '...the spiritual facul-

---

[77]   AN 6.64

ties of other beings...' '...the defilement, cleansing, and emergence of jhānas, liberations, samādhi, and attainments...' 'I recollect various past lives...' 'I understand with the divine eye how beings pass on according to their actions...' 'I enter and abide, due to the evaporation of the poisons, in the poison-free release of heart, release by understanding, having witnessed it here & now with my own direct knowledge.'[78]

Insight 4: Independence

210   The insight section of the Satipaṭṭhāna Sutta concludes with the following statement:

211   'One abides independent, not grasping at anything in the world.'[79]

212   For advanced practitioners this is taught as the comprehensive detachment from any aspect of existence.[80] But another aspect of 'independence' is particularly relevant to stream-entry.

213   'The four satipaṭṭhānas are taught and described by me for the abandoning and surmounting of these dependencies on views connected with former times and dependencies on views connected with times to come.'[81]

214   This passage makes an direct link between the practice of satipaṭṭhāna and the overcoming of views. The views connected with the past concern the idea of a 'self' as providing a link between this life and previous lives, which views of the future concern future lives. In other words, if we think

---

[78] SN 52.6, 11–24
[79] MN 10.5*ff.*, DN 22.2*ff.*
[80] E.g. MN 143
[81] DN 29.40

of our 'self' as an identical, unchanging essence, then in understanding the past we will naturally postulate that this very same 'self' existed in past lives, and will exist in future lives.

215   Thinking in this way will obscure the true nature of conditions, the fact that, even here & now, we are constantly changing and altering with conditions, so how much more so in the past and the future? The reality is that all experience in the past or future is based on the same conditional principles that may be observed here in the present. Hence an understanding of past and future lives comes not from a metaphysical theory of a 'self', but by observing the changing nature of consciousness according to dependent origination.

216   'All these contemplatives and brahmans who hold settled views about the past and the future, and assert on sixty-two grounds various conceptual theorems referring to the past and the future, experience these feelings only by repeated contacts through the six bases of contact. Due to feeling as condition, there arises in them craving. Due to craving as condition, there is grasping. Due to grasping as condition, there is [ongoing] existence. Due to existence as condition, there is birth. Due to birth as condition, aging & death, sorrow, lamentation, bodily pain, mental suffering, and despair come to be. When a monk understands in accordance with reality the origin, ending, gratification, danger, and escape regarding the six bases of contact, then he understands what lies beyond all these views.'[82]

217   In this passage, views are traced to an innocuous origin in the very process of sense perception. 'Contact' is where the

---

[82] DN 1.144

inner and outer meet; the interface of the self and the world. That moment is not a neutral record of data, as for example a camera. All we see, hear, sense, is interpreted, classified, sorted out by the mind; and crucially, we either like or dislike or are neutral. This sets up the dynamic of the mind that moves, pulled this way and that by sense experience. Our craving and desire grows, and we form various theories of identification, such as by saying, 'This is mine, this is not mine'. Through this process our attachment to rebirth propels us on to life after life.

218   Views of 'self' in the past and future are classified by Buddhism as 'annihilationism' and 'eternalism'. Each of these classes of views encompasses many variations. But the most familiar form of annihilationism is the belief that this physical realm is all there is, and after death there is no other life. Eternalism typically postulates an everlasting soul that survives death and lives forever in a blissful—or painful—state. According to the Buddha, these are extreme views, neither of which does justice to the complexity and nuance of reality as we experience it.

219   Never in our life to we actually experience a moment of consciousness that actually ends, with nothing coming after. Since this is simply not part of our experience, how can we insist that this is what happens after death? Similarly, never do we experience a state of permanence or eternity, nor can we even imagine what such a state might be. Both of these views fail the simple test of Buddhist empiricism: can they be reasonably inferred from actual experience?

220   Life involves both change and continuity, both unity and diversity. Buddhist philosophy accepts both of these aspects, and insists that they cannot be taken as absolutes.

221   This twofold philosophical approach calls for a twofold meditative response: samatha and vipassanā. Samatha is a joyous plunge into oneness, the inner waters of the mind. When we experience the ending of the five external senses, we can no longer believe that only externals are real, and will turn away from annihilationism. Vipassanā discloses the radical discontinuity of consciousness, dispelling the belief in an eternal soul.

222   Since it is only suffering that ceases, the gradual stilling of activities is experienced as exquisite bliss by the meditator. One can at last be truly independent, as one experiences for oneself the fading away of suffering. Faith in this process of peace enables the meditator to loosen, then untie the shackles binding the mind to the world, free of the fear that there could be any kind of existing 'self' to be destroyed. This is the right view of the stream-enterer.

223
> 'Activities are impermanent,
> Their nature's to rise and fall.
> Having arisen, they cease:
> Their stilling is bliss.'[83]

Conclusion: Satipaṭṭhāna and Insight

224   Contemplation of rise and fall refers not to an objective, pseudo-scientific scrutiny of phenomena 'out there', independent of the observer, but to seeing the way the mind entangles itself in the world, altering what is known by the very act of knowing. This implies that it is the understanding of the mind itself, the faculty of knowing, which is the crucial element in the delicate process of disentanglement. Mind consciousness is the resort of the five senses,

---

[83]   DN 16.6.10 etc.

the functional center coordinating experience, and the subjective sense of individual identity linking life to life. While
samādhi plays an important role in all aspects of insight,
its 'home base' is the contemplation of mind. So samādhi is
the straight road from virtue to wisdom, focusing attention
right at the heart of the matter and providing a perspective
for the other aspects of insight.

The Bases of Psychic Power

225 These are: enthusiasm, energy, mind, and inquiry.

226 'Dependent on enthusiasm [... energy... mind... in-
quiry], one gains samādhi, one gains one-pointedness
of mind; when endowed with active striving, this is
the base of psychic power consisting of enthusiasm
[... energy... mind... inquiry].'[84]

227 Thus these are various mental qualities which predomi-
nate in gaining samādhi. 'Enthusiasm' is a wholesome mode
of desire; not the worldly desire to 'be' or 'have', but especially in this context of samādhi, the desire to know. Both enthusiasm and energy are compassed within the path factor
of right effort in its role as 'requisite of samādhi'. 'Inquiry'
is wisdom in its mode of investigation into the reasons for
progress or decline in meditation. 'Mind' here denotes samādhi itself. The word 'mind' (*citta*) is a common synonym for
samādhi. It is not defined further here, but as it is a basis for
psychic power, there is no doubt as to the meaning.

228 'That a monk without refined, peaceful, tranquil,
and unified samādhi could wield the various kinds

---

[84] SN 51.13 condensed

of psychic power... or witness the evaporation of the poisons: that is not possible.'[85]

229   An interesting analysis details the manner of developing all four of these factors.

230   'Here, monks, a monk develops the basis of psychic power consisting of samādhi due to enthusiasm [... energy... mind... inquiry] and active striving, thinking: "Thus my enthusiasm will be neither too slack nor too tense, and it will neither be constricted within [due to sloth & torpor] nor distracted externally [due to sense pleasures]." He abides perceiving before and after: "As before, so after; as after, so before; as below, so above; as above, so below; as by day, so by night; as by night, so by day." Thus with heart open and unenveloped, he develops a mind imbued with luminosity.'[86]

231   'As below, so above' is explained in the sutta with reference to the meditation on the parts of the body 'upwards from the soles of the feet, and downwards from the tips of the hairs'. 'As before, so after' probably refers to evenness in attending to the meditation subject throughout the session. The phrase 'well apprehended, well attended, well borne in mind, well penetrated with understanding' is used here just as with the 'basis for reviewing', implying that reviewing and inquiring into causes is a key to developing this evenness.

232   This inquiry will investigate the causal relationships between the bases of psychic power themselves, in line with similar relationships described elsewhere. Enthusiasm is the wish, the motivation to do the work of purifying the mind. Effort is the actual exerting of energy to do the work. The purified mind is the result of that work. And in the clar-

---

[85]   AN 6.70
[86]   SN 51.20

ity of the purified mind, the causes and conditions for that purity can be discerned through inquiry.

233   These qualities work together like an electric light. Enthusiasm is like the voltage in the circuits. Energy is like the current of electricity which flows when the switch is turned on. The mind is like the globe lighting up. And when the room is lit, it's easy to see what is there.

Spiritual Faculties & Powers

234   The spiritual faculties and powers are simply different aspects of the same set of principles,[87] which are: faith, energy, mindfulness, samādhi, and understanding. Here is one description of how they work together.

235   'Bhante, a noble disciple who is absolutely dedicated to the Tathāgata, with full confidence would not doubt or be uncertain about the Tathāgata or the Tathāgata's dispensation. It is to be expected, Bhante, of a faithful noble disciple that he will abide with energy aroused for the abandoning of unbeneficial qualities and the undertaking of beneficial qualities, that he will be strong, firm in exertion, not shirking his responsibility regarding beneficial qualities. His energy is his spiritual faculty of energy.

236   'It is to be expected, Bhante, of a faithful noble disciple whose energy is aroused that he will be mindful, endowed with supreme mindfulness and mastery [over the senses], able to remember and recall what was said and done long ago. His mindfulness is his spiritual faculty of mindfulness.

237   'It is to be expected, Bhante, of a faithful noble disciple whose energy is aroused and whose mindful-

---

[87] SN 48.43

ness is established that, having made relinquishment
the support, he will gain samādhi, he will gain one-
pointedness of mind. His samādhi is his spiritual faculty of samādhi.

238   'It is to be expected, Bhante, of a faithful noble disciple whose energy is aroused, whose mindfulness is established and whose mind is concentrated in samādhi
that he will understand: "Inconceivable is saṁsāra's
beginning. For beings hindered by ignorance and fettered by craving, a starting point of roaming on and
faring on is not found. But the remainderless fading
away and cessation of that dark mass of ignorance—
that state is peaceful, that state is sublime, that is, the
samatha of all activities, the relinquishment of all belongings, the evaporation of craving, fading away, cessation, Nibbana." His understanding is his spiritual
faculty of understanding.

239   'That faithful noble disciple, having thus repeatedly
practiced striving, remembering, samādhi, and understanding has full confidence thus: "These principles which I had previously only heard about I now
abide having personally contacted, and see having penetrated with understanding."'[88]

240   These principles are conveniently elaborated in groups
of four, bringing them in line with the corresponding path-
factors: faith should be seen in the four factors of stream-
entry (faith in the Buddha, Dhamma, Sangha, and perfect
virtue); energy in the four right efforts; mindfulness in the
four satipaṭṭhānas; samādhi in the four jhānas; and understanding in the four noble truths.[89] However, understanding
is most commonly defined as 'the noble and penetrative un-

[88]   SN 48.50
[89]   SN 48.8

derstanding of arising and ending which leads to the complete evaporation of suffering.'[90]

241   The phrase 'having made relinquishment the support, one gains samādhi' is unique to the spiritual faculties. The precise meaning may be read a number of ways, which I discuss further below. However we read this, it should not be seen as an alternative to jhana, since the phrase itself is sometimes followed by the full jhāna formula.[91]

242   The spiritual powers are defined similarly, the sole difference being the absence of the phrase 'having made relinquishment the support.'[92] Since the spiritual faculties and powers are identical, that phrase cannot add anything crucial to the definition, or justify extending the scope of the spiritual faculty of samādhi beyond the four jhānas.

243   Each of the spiritual faculties and powers are further described as being developed together with each of the four jhānas.[93] One practicing in this way, even for the duration of a finger snap, 'does the Teacher's bidding, responds to instruction, and does not waste the nation's almsfood.'

244   Strikingly, the texts set the spiritual faculties apart from the other sets comprised within the wings to awakening by treating them under all four of the noble truths, not just the fourth.[94] Normally, of course, all these groups are considered to fall under the topic of the Path as the fourth noble truth. By treating the spiritual faculties under all four noble

---

[90] SN 48.9

[91] SN 48.10

[92] AN 7.4, AN 5.14, AN 5.15

[93] AN 1.20

[94] SN 48.2-7. This treatment foreshadows the terminological development, already nascent in the suttas, of 'faculty' as a general phenomenological classification parallel to the aggregates, sense bases, and elements.

truths, the suttas invite us to contemplate that the path, too, is conditioned, impermanent, and still subject to suffering. This is the task of the spiritual faculty of understanding itself, defined precisely as understanding rise and fall.

245   So to possess the faculties, one must understand the faculties. The faculties should be seen as arising dependent on each other, and this interdependence shows how the mind works, not just in the context of the spiritual faculties, but in everything. The one who perfects this 'understanding in accordance with reality' is the stream-enterer.[95]

246   Hence, although as mental qualities they are to be developed by the ordinary person, only with the entrance to the noble path do they gain control, becoming the predominating dispositions in their own field, thus meriting the title 'spiritual faculties'.[96]

247   Not only does the presence or absence of the spiritual faculties serve to distinguish between the ordinary person and the noble ones, the relative strength of the faculties is a key criterion for classifying the noble ones in terms of spiritual potential, level of attainment, and mode of practice.

248   To return to the obscure phrase, 'having made relinquishment the support', we should consider this in light of such passages as the following, which describe how the noble ones meditate. In this passage, 'taints of the mind' does not refer, as elsewhere, to the five hindrances, but to the manifestations of greed, anger, and delusion abandoned by the stages of the noble path.

249   'When he has given up, expelled, released, abandoned, and relinquished [the taints of the mind] in

---

[95] E.g. SN 48.2, 3; see too SN 22.109, M2.11, etc.
[96] MN 26.21. Although the term 'spiritual faculties' may be used in a more general sense, this is not identified with the group of five.

part, he thinks: "I am endowed with confirmed confidence in the Buddha [... Dhamma... Sangha]." He gains inspiration in the meaning, inspiration in the Dhamma, gladness connected with the Dhamma. In one who is glad, rapture is born. In one whose mind is rapturous, the body becomes tranquil. One with tranquil body feels bliss. The mind of one who is blissful enters samādhi.'[97]

250 This passage describes how someone who has already reached at least stream-entry finds joy in this fact; this joy and lightness of heart at having overcome some of the deepest afflictions of the mind itself becomes the foundation for gaining samādhi.

251 'Confirmed confidence' is the clarity from having undergone the experience of forever relinquishing defilements, thereby walking in the Buddha's footsteps, seeing the Dhamma, and becoming one of the noble Sangha. Here, the spiritual faculty of faith is predominant in the meditation subject of recollecting the Triple Gem; energy is implied in the undertaking of meditation; while mindfulness is the act of recollecting. Samādhi here is obviously 'noble right samādhi', equivalent to the spiritual faculty of samādhi.

252 The word for 'relinquishment' (*paṭinissagga*) is a slightly different form than in the spiritual faculty of samādhi (*vossagga*), but the meaning is surely the same. If we are on the right track, then it would seem that the reason why the unique phrase 'having made relinquishment the support' appears before the jhāna formula in the definition of the spiritual faculty of samādhi is linked to the fact that only the noble ones actually possess the spiritual faculties in the true sense. Only they have their course of medita-

---

[97] MN 7.8

253 tion smoothed by the root-level eradication of defilements. Supported by the relinquishment of defilements, it is much easier for them to gain samādhi.

In the above sutta, the monk next develops the divine abidings, and then the sutta shows how the highest wisdom is attained:

254 'He understands thus: "There is this, there is the inferior, there is the superior, and beyond there is an escape from this whole field of perception."'

255 As so often in the suttas, this laconic phrase appears almost willfully obscure. But the phrase 'field of perception' invites comparison with such passages as the Poṭṭhapāda Sutta, which then offers a key to interpretation.[98] 'This' refers to the divine abidings; 'the inferior' to the sensual realm; 'the superior' to the formless liberations; while 'the escape' is Nibbana. So the spiritual faculties, relying on the partial relinquishment of defilements by the trainees, mature into the total relinquishment of defilements by the arahant.

The Enlightenment Factors

256 'They lead to enlightenment, therefore they are called enlightenment factors.'[99]

257 The seven enlightenment factors are: mindfulness, investigation of dhammas, energy, rapture, tranquility, samādhi, and equanimity. Generally, they may be regarded as a presentation of the meditative aspect of the path, complementary to the bases for psychic powers and the spiritual faculties. The very first sutta of the collection on the enlightenment

---

[98] DN 9.10*ff.* quoted below. See too Iti 72, 73.
[99] SN 46.5

factors, however, emphasizes the indispensability of virtuous ethical conduct as their foundation.[100]

258   'Mindfulness' and 'investigation of dhammas', include both the recollection and investigation of teachings as well as the discriminative contemplation of presently arisen mental phenomena. 'Energy' and 'tranquility' include both physical and mental aspects. 'Rapture' and 'samādhi' occur either with initial & sustained application of mind (in the first jhāna) or without (in the higher jhānas). 'Equanimity' is the crowning quality of samatha, reaching perfection in the fourth jhāna and the fourth divine abiding.

259   A whole series of texts deal with the opposition between the enlightenment factors and the five hindrances. This is presented both as a general appraisal of the two sets as leading to or obstructing enlightenment, and as a specific analysis, especially in terms of the distinctive 'nutriment' for each factor. The gradual assimilation of the nutriments through repeated attention nurtures the growth of either good or bad qualities.

260   Sometimes a specific enlightenment factor opposes a specific hindrance. The nutriment for 'investigation of dhammas'—discriminating between good and bad—starves the hindrance of doubt. The nutriments of energy—the elements of arousal, of exertion, of persistence—starve the hindrance of sloth & torpor. Tranquility opposes restlessness & remorse. Samādhi is nurtured by those things that are 'the basis of samatha, the basis of non-dispersal'.[101]

261   The suttas do not directly oppose samādhi and rapture to particular hindrances, but elsewhere the commentaries set them against sensual desire and ill will respectively. Equa-

---

[100] SN 46.1
[101] SN 46.51

nimity, along with tranquility and samādhi, serves to pacify
the excited mind, whereas investigation, energy, and rapture rouse up the sluggish mind. Mindfulness is always useful. Mindfulness, rapture, and equanimity are not allocated
specific nutriments; perhaps the Buddha is throwing us back
on our own 'investigation of dhammas' to discern these.

262   Each of the enlightenment factors may be developed in
conjunction with various meditation subjects: a skeleton; a
decaying corpse; the divine abidings; mindfulness of breathing; and the perceptions of ugliness, death, the repulsive-
ness of food, boredom with the whole world, impermanence,
suffering, not-self, abandonment, fading away, and cessation. Developed in this way, these meditations are of great
fruit and benefit, lead to arahantship or non-returning, to
great good, security from bondage, a sense of urgency, and
a comfortable abiding.[102]

263   One passage describes how the enlightenment factors
arise through recollecting the Dhamma of the noble ones.
Here, 'spiritual rapture' seems to encompass rapture arisen
prior to jhāna, but only, of course, as a prelude to jhāna, not
as a replacement for it.

264   'On an occasion when a monk abiding withdrawn
       remembers and thinks over that Dhamma, the enlight-
       enment factor of mindfulness is aroused, developed,
       and fulfilled. Abiding thus mindfully, he investigates,
       explores, and inquires into that Dhamma with under-
       standing... His energy is roused up and persistent...
       Spiritual rapture arises... In one who is rapturous, the
       body and mind become tranquil... In one whose body
       is tranquil, there is bliss. The mind of one whose body
       is tranquil and who is blissful enters samādhi... One
       watches closely with equanimity the mind thus con-

---

[102] SN 46.57ff.

centrated in samādhi.' [Thus all the factors of enlightenment are roused, developed, and fulfilled.][103]

265   Samatha and vipassanā are intimately interlaced through
all these teachings. It is noteworthy, though, that most of
these factors pertain to samatha, while only investigation of
dhammas pertains specifically to vipassanā, and even this
is chiefly treated in its mode of supporting samādhi. Indeed,
these seven dhammas sometimes simply substitute for samādhi in the grouping: virtue, dhamma, understanding.[104] The
emphasis throughout is simply on the development of the
mind. Many terms used with these principles—'seclusion',
'fading away', 'cessation', 'relinquishment', 'abandoning',
'ending', 'stilling', and others—are also used of the four jhānas, vipassanā, and even Nibbana itself, underlining the
essential kinship of these facets of the path and the goal.

The Wings to Enlightenment: A Conclusion

266   Examining these thirty-seven wings to enlightenment,
consistent patterns emerge. The sequences start with more
basic qualities: faith, or enthusiasm, or energy. The placing

---

[103] SN 46.3

[104] This grouping occurs several times in the suttas, usually glossed by the
commentary as 'dhammas pertaining to samādhi', but as far as I know
only explained in the suttas at Iti 3.97 as 'the seven dhammas that are
wings to enlightenment', which is often translated as 'the seven sets
of dhammas that are wings to enlightenment'. Now it is well known
that the thirty-seven are not called 'wings to enlightenment' in the
suttas. The term is used of the spiritual faculties, however, and as there
are many descriptive terms common to both the spiritual faculties
and the enlightenment factors, I feel it would be easier for an epithet
to transfer from one set to another than from one set to the whole
group of sets. Moreover, 'dhamma' is more idiomatically used of the
members of the set rather than the set as a whole.

of investigation of dhammas near the start of the enlightenment factors is reminiscent of the placing of right view
at the start of the eightfold path. With energy and mindfulness in operation, the mind develops the joy which leads
to samādhi, ripening in liberating wisdom. Fundamental
principles of the nature of the mind are embodied in these
formulations. At each stage the emotional and intellectual
qualities are balanced and support each other, while the
variations warn against taking an overly rigid approach to
development. In the next chapter we will examine in more
detail the relationships between these qualities.

267   'Thus, Ānanda, beneficial virtues gradually proceed
to the peak.'[105]

---

[105] AN 10.1

Chapter 4

Dependent Liberation

'Monks, one who is virtuous need not wish: "May I be free from remorse." It is natural that the virtuous are free from remorse.

'One who is free from remorse need not wish: "May I be glad." It is natural that in one free from remorse, gladness arises.

'One who is glad need not wish: "May I feel rapture." It is natural that one who is glad feels rapture.

'One who feels rapture need not wish: "May my body be tranquil." It is natural that one who feels rapture has a tranquil body.

'One whose body is tranquil need not wish: "May I feel bliss." It is natural that one whose body is tranquil feels bliss.

'One who is blissful need not wish: "May my mind be concentrated in samādhi." It is natural that one who is blissful has samādhi.

'One who has samādhi need not wish: "May I know & see in line with reality." It is natural that one who has samādhi knows & sees in line with reality.

'One who knows & sees in line with reality need not wish: "May I be repulsed." It is natural that one who knows & sees is repulsed.

'One who is repulsed need not wish: "May lust fade away." It is natural that lust fades away in one who is repulsed.

'One whose lust has faded away need not wish: "May I witness the knowledge & vision of release." It is natural that one whose lust has faded away witnesses the knowledge & vision of release...

'Thus, monks, dhammas flow on to and fulfill dhammas for crossing over from the near to the far shore.'

— THE BUDDHA, AN 11.2

Causality

ENLIGHTENMENT IS NO ACCIDENT. It emerges from a precisely defined set of conditions, which are frequently depicted in the suttas. There is no widely used term for this doctrinal framework, so I have coined the term 'dependent liberation'.[1] Many versions occur in the suttas, but with a common pattern, displaying the conditional unfolding of liberation as an evolution of ever more refined qualities. All of the variations follow the sequence virtue, samādhi, wisdom. Often these broad categories are subdivided, revealing their inner structure as comprised of further conditional sequences. Such passages as the above, which treat the samādhi section in most detail, occur throughout the suttas.

---

[1]   Elsewhere it has been called 'transcendental dependent origination'.

2   Some understanding of the principles of causality is essential to fully appreciate the significance of this teaching. Causes can be analyzed as two kinds: necessary conditions and sufficient conditions. A necessary condition is one whose absence makes it impossible for the result to occur. For example, a necessary condition for being a woman is being a human being; if one is not a human being, it is impossible to be a woman. A sufficient condition is one whose presence makes it inevitable that the result will occur. For example, a sufficient condition for being a human being is being a woman; if one is a woman, it definitely follows that one is a human being.

3   The two need not, as in the examples above, be exclusive. For example, a necessary and sufficient condition for being a human being is being a featherless biped; if one is not a featherless biped, one cannot be a human being and if one is a featherless biped, it definitely follows that one is a human being. Or a condition may be neither necessary nor sufficient. For example, being a boy is neither necessary nor sufficient condition for becoming an adult human being, but merely conducive.

4   This distinction is critical. If in the thought-world of the suttas 'x is a condition for y' means 'x is a sufficient condition for y', this leaves open the question whether other things may also be sufficient. Virtue, samādhi, and understanding lead to Nibbana; but there may be another, or a myriad of other paths up the same mountain. If however, 'x is a condition for y' means 'x is a necessary condition for y', we must regard all 'x'—each of the factors subsumed within such a causal relationship—as being indispensable.

5   So which alternative applies in the sutta teachings on causality? Let us start with the most general formula for

causality in dependent origination, known as 'specific conditionality':[2]

6   'When this exists, that is; due to the arising of this,
that arises.

7   'When this does not exist, that is not; due to the
cessation of this, that ceases.'

8   The first pair of principles appears to imply sufficient conditionality. If something exists, another thing comes to be.
However, a close contextual examination reveals that this
is not so. Here is one example where someone possessed of
an earlier condition for spiritual progress, ethical conduct,
does not realize the higher states.

9   'That noble disciple, content with the virtues beloved
of the noble ones, does not try further for seclusion by
day and retreat by night. Abiding thus negligent, gladness does not arise. When there is no gladness, there
is no rapture. When there is no rapture, there is no
tranquility. When there is no tranquility, he abides in
suffering. The mind of one who suffers does not enter
samādhi. Dhammas do not manifest in a mind without samādhi. Because dhammas do not manifest he is
called an abider in negligence.'[3]

10   If such sequences were based on a concept of sufficient
conditionality, there would be no point in making an effort,
for an ethical person would naturally gain samādhi, whether
or not they actually meditated.

11   This is not an isolated example. In the standard sequence
of dependent origination, it is said that 'feeling is the condition for craving'. If 'feeling' were a sufficient condition
for 'craving', then no-one, including the Buddha, would be

---

[2]   SN 12.37 etc.
[3]   SN 55.40

exempt from craving. All spiritual practice would be ineffectual.

12   There are in fact many conditions left unstated in these contexts. It is fundamental to Buddhist causality that many factors are present at all times, interacting in complex ways. The suttas do not claim to offer a complete analysis of every factor at all times; rather, they point to what is useful, what is necessary.

13   In the context of practice, the notion of sufficient condition applies only in that a noble disciple must eventually attain liberation even if, as above, they are 'mightily negligent'.[4]

14   If the main causal connections spoken of in Buddhism are not 'sufficient conditions', then should they be seen as 'necessary conditions'? The relation of 'necessity' is, in fact, one that is specified in many passages. Here is one example, in the context of dependent origination:

15   'If there were not the birth of those various kinds of beings into the various states [of existence]; when all kinds of birth do not exist, due to the cessation of birth, would aging & death be found?'

16   'No Bhante.'[5]

17   Quite clearly, birth is a necessary condition for aging & death. It is true that birth is also a sufficient condition for death; however it is not a sufficient condition for aging (because a being who has been newly born might die immediately before aging). So the notion of sufficiency cannot be inherent in the causal specification; it must be inferred from context.

---

[4]   Snp 230
[5]   DN 15.4

18   Below we shall see the kinship between dependent origination and dependent liberation, like an image and its reflection, expressed in various ways in the suttas. And just
as causality in dependent origination is primarily necessary conditionality, all the main similes illustrating dependent liberation likewise imply necessity—the rain filling
the mountain streams, the leaves sustaining the tree, or each
stage of a journey bringing one to the next.[6] This means that
these passages embody an invariable law of nature: unless
these conditions are fulfilled, it is impossible that the result
can occur.

19   Our first passage above, however, shows a more active
process than mere necessity. The previous conditions do
not merely allow subsequent conditions to arise, they are
an energy that actively promotes the arising. The main emphasis is not that the absence of the conditions immediately destroys the resultant phenomena, but that without
the supporting conditions the results are not nourished to
fulfillment. Although this does not apply to all causal relationships found in the suttas, it is an important aspect of
the contexts dealing with practice—they have a direction,
a forward impetus. Following the way of the world, the sequence of dependent origination starting with ignorance,
one is swept along the stream of birth, aging, and death. But
the sequence starting with faith and virtue will sweep one
along to Nibbana.

20   Some writers have tried to reduce Buddhist conditionality
to the 'mutuality condition', that is, when two factors act
as a mutual support for each other, as when two sheaves of
straw lean against one another. If all Buddhist conditions

---

[6]   Similar similes are applied to dependent origination at SN 12.23,
SN 12.55, SN 12.69.

were mutual, then this would apply to samatha and vipassanā as well—they would be entirely equal partners. But this type of condition, though important, is restricted to a few contexts. In many contexts, this relation is expressly denied.[7] It would be difficult to establish from the suttas that the normal expressions for conditional relations can mean, in and of themselves, 'conascent' (or 'mutuality') condition. The few occasions where such a relation is discussed emphasize how abstruse and unusual this was regarded.[8] And even here the standard conditional clause does not alone bear the burden of expressing two-way conditionality. Conascence is explained instead with two separate mirror-image statements of one-way conditionality.

21   This lack of full mutuality is emphasized in the relationship between samādhi and wisdom. In the Poṭṭhapāda Sutta, the Buddha first describes 'perception' in terms of the successive refinement of perception through the jhānas leading to insight knowledge. This passage deals with the relation between perception—how things *seem*—which arises in samādhi, and knowledge—how things *are*—which is vipassanā.

22   'But Bhante, does perception arise first and knowledge afterwards, or does knowledge arise first and perception afterwards?'

23   'Perception, Poṭṭhapāda, arises first, knowledge afterwards; due to the arising of perception there is the arising of knowledge. One understands thus: "It seems that my knowledge arose due to that condition."'[9]

24   In this kind of relationship, the earlier quality is a necessary condition for the later; the later quality can then support and reinforce the earlier developed quality. But it is

---

7   SN 14.3, 5, 8, 10
8   E.g. DN 15.21–22, SN 12.67, MN 43.22
9   DN 9.20; see below.

never in a fully mutual or equal relationship. This is like a mother's relationship with her child. A child as they mature may give their mother as much support and help as they are able, but can never repay the gift of life. Similarly, wisdom can act as a supporting condition to deepen clarity of awareness, but can only see its way to do so dependent on clarity already present. So although, as we have said again and again, these two qualities are closely connected and mutually supportive, it is nevertheless the case that samādhi is, in the final analysis, preliminary to the wisdom of realization.

25   Still, wisdom can, and indeed must, be developed from the beginning of practice. Three main modes of the wisdom which precedes samādhi can be discerned. Firstly, conceptual understanding from hearing and reflecting on the teachings. Second, investigation into the causes of samādhi. Third, vipassanā proper—the clear-eyed discernment of conditioned reality.

26   Now obviously these three aspects are closely linked, and the mention of any one of them is a particular context should normally understood by way of emphasis, not exclusion. A thread unifying all these modes is that wisdom is described in some sort of relation to samādhi, not apart from it. This initial understanding helps to prepare the mind, but only with the ripening of the other path factors does it mature into the wisdom that really counts, 'knowledge & vision in accordance with reality'.

27   'It is, monks, just like a house with a peaked roof. As long as the roof peak has not been set in place, the rafters are not steady, not stable. But when the roof peak has been set in place, then the rafters are steady and stable. So too, as long as noble knowledge has not arisen in the noble disciple, the [other] four spiritual

faculties are not steady, not stable. But when noble
knowledge has arisen in the noble disciple, the [other]
four spiritual faculties are steady and stable.'[10]

28   The rafters of faith, energy, mindfulness, and samādhi
must be set up before the roof peak of noble understanding can be set in place. They are the necessary antecedent
conditions for liberating wisdom. Understanding in its turn
fortifies and firmly fixes the four already existing faculties.
This kind of 'feedback loop' may have quite a general application—any subsequent quality can strengthen previously
developed qualities. However, this should not distract from
the prevailing paradigm of sequential conditions. Hence the
suttas state quite clearly:

29   'That one could fulfill the aggregate of understanding without having fulfilled the aggregate of samādhi:
that is not possible.'[11]

30   There is no equivalent passage stating that development of
understanding must be fulfilled before one gains samādhi.

31   These considerations point to an understanding of causality that is definite and structured. The Buddha did not teach
causality with such philosophical pleasantries as 'Everything is interrelated.' He taught specific conditionality—
this is the cause of *that*. The same patterns occur over and
over. Craving is the cause of suffering; but just as the lotus grows in the mud, the experience of suffering is the
essential motivation for the spiritual practice which will
end suffering.

32   In the Upanisā Sutta, the connection between the normal dependent origination and the liberating sequence is

[10]   SN 48.52
[11]   AN 5.22

made explicit.[12] The sequence starts out as usual with ignorance leading up to birth and suffering; but suffering gives rise not to despair, but to faith. This emotional conviction then triggers the same sequence of joy, rapture, tranquility, bliss, samādhi, insight, and release that was described above beginning with virtue.[13] The sequence of twelve factors, beginning with suffering, is the positive counterpart of the twelve factors of the cessation mode of the normal dependent origination. Intriguingly, dependent origination in the mode of origination is called 'the wrong way of practice', just as the wrong eightfold path, while the mode of cessation is called 'the right way of practice', just as the right eightfold path. This collapses the distinction between theory and practice, between the middle teaching and the middle way.[14]

The Mahā Nidāna Sutta also describes the ending of suffering in positive terms, by focusing on two kinds of arahants.[15] The first is 'released by understanding'. Here this is described as understanding the origin, ending, gratification, danger, and escape in the case of the seven stations of consciousness and two bases. These are all planes into which rebirth can occur depending on the level of development of consciousness, with particular emphasis on meditative attainments. Here the identity is clear between consciousness as a link in dependent origination, as the mind states developed in meditation, and as the stream of consciousness flowing on to rebirth in the various worlds. The second kind of arahant is the 'both-sides released', who is distinguished by fluency in all the meditative attainments. Thus

---

[12] SN 12.23

[13] In the spiritual faculties, virtue is included in faith. SN 48.8 cp. SN 55.3, etc.

[14] SN 12.3, SN 45.23

[15] DN 15.33*ff.*

the transparent mind of samādhi has a key role throughout in unraveling the tangle of saṁsāra.

34   'This dependent origination is profound, and appears profound. Not awakening to and not penetrating this principle, this generation has become like a tangled ball of string, matted like a bird's nest, entangled like a mass of coarse grass, and does not evolve beyond lower realms, bad destinies, the abyss, and saṁsāra.'[16]

35   A tangled ball of string will never untie itself, and so too the mind entangled in worldly affairs will never loosen the knot of suffering. The key difference between enlightened and unenlightened beings is their sincerity of devotion to spiritual practice.

36   'For the fool [as for the sage], hindered by ignorance and fettered by craving, this [conscious] body has been acquired. Thus there is the duality of this body and external mentality & physical form. Dependent on this duality, there is contact. There are just six sense bases, contacted through which—or through one of them— the fool [and the sage] experience pleasure and pain. What then is the difference, the distinction, between the fool and the sage?'...

37   'For the fool, this ignorance has not been abandoned and this craving has not been evaporated. For what reason? Because the fool has not lived the holy life for the complete evaporation of suffering. Therefore with the breaking up of the body, the fool passes on to a [new] body. He is not released from birth, aging, death, sorrow, lamentation, bodily pain, mental suffering, and despair; he is not released from suffering, I say.

38   'But for the sage, this ignorance has been abandoned and this craving has been evaporated. For what rea-

---

[16] DN 15.1

son? Because the sage has lived the holy life for the complete evaporation of suffering. Therefore with the breaking up of the body, the sage does not pass on to a [new] body. He is released from birth, aging, death, sorrow, lamentation, bodily pain, mental suffering, and despair; he is released from suffering, I say.

39   'This is the distinction, the difference, between the fool and the sage, that is, living the holy life.'[17]

40   'The holy life' is usually identified as the noble eightfold path.[18] Its application in this context is illustrated in the Mahātaṇhāsaṅkhaya Sutta. This is one of the most important discourses on dependent origination, set up specifically to refute the view that it is this 'very same consciousness' that fares on through the round of rebirths. It is one of the contexts which suggests that the word 'consciousness' was established pre-Buddhist parlance for the principle underlying rebirth. As he often did, the Buddha accepted the conventional terminology but redefined it, insisting that consciousness arises according to conditions.

41   The Buddha also takes over a brahmanical view that reincarnation of the embryo occurs concurrent with three things: the coming together of the mother and father; the mother is fertile; and the being to be reborn is present.[19] Having taken rebirth, one is nourished by the mother, plays childish games, and, as the sense faculties mature, engages in favoring and opposing feelings, giving rise to craving and future rebirth. The round of cessation is shown with the full gradual training, from the appearance of the Tathāgata and the going forth, to the abandoning of the hindrances.

---

[17]   SN 12.19

[18]   SN 45.39

[19]   See MN 93.18

42   'Having thus abandoned these five hindrances, taints
of the mind which rob understanding of its strength...
he enters and abides in the first jhāna... second jhāna...
third jhāna... fourth jhāna. Seeing a visible form with
the eye, he does not lust for pleasant seeming visible
forms. He abides with mindfulness of the body established, with an immeasurable heart, and he understands in accordance with reality the release of heart,
release by understanding where these evil unbeneficial phenomena cease without remainder. Having
thus abandoned favoring and opposing, whatever feeling he feels, whether pleasant, or painful, or neither
pleasant nor painful, he does not relish, welcome, or
remain attached to it... The relishing of feelings ceases
in him. Due to the cessation of his relishing, grasping
ceases. Due to the cessation of grasping, [ongoing] existence ceases. Due to the cessation of existence, birth
ceases. Due to the cessation of birth, aging & death,
sorrow, lamentation, bodily pain, mental suffering,
and despair cease. Thus there is the cessation of this
whole mass of suffering. [And so on for the ear, etc.]'[20]

43   Something of the profound relationship between the evolving sequence of dhammas beginning with faith or virtue
and the core of the Dhamma is beginning to emerge, how
this process is both necessary for and powerfully inducive
to liberation. I have coined the term 'vital condition' to bring
out these two aspects.

44   'Monks, when there is no mindfulness and clear
comprehension, in one without mindfulness and clear
comprehension, the vital condition for conscience and
fear of wrong-doing is destroyed.

---

[20] MN 38

45   'When there is no conscience and fear of wrong-doing... the vital condition for sense restraint is destroyed.

46   'When there is no sense restraint... the vital condition for virtue is destroyed.

47   'When there is no virtue... the vital condition for right samādhi is destroyed.

48   'When there is no right samādhi, in one without right samādhi, the vital condition for knowledge & vision in accordance with reality is destroyed.

49   'When there is no knowledge & vision in accordance with reality... the vital condition for repulsion and fading away is destroyed.

50   'When there is no repulsion and fading away... the vital condition for knowledge & vision of release is destroyed.

51   'Just as, monks, when a tree is without leaves and twigs, the branches, bark, sapwood, and heartwood do not come to fulfillment...'[21]

52   The critical link here is between 'right samādhi' (= jhāna) and 'knowledge & vision in accordance with reality'. This phrase refers to the stream-enterer's 'vision of the Dhamma'. In other words, this passages says that jhāna is a necessary condition for stream-entry.[22]

53   It is quite striking that in this, as well as many other passages, there is no clear mention of vipassanā. The commentaries treat 'knowledge & vision in accordance with reality' as immature vipassanā. But this cannot be so, since immature vipassanā may be developed prior to jhāna, whereas here we are told that jhāna is a vital condition. Vipassanā

---

[21] AN 8.81; cp. AN 5.24, AN 5.168, AN 6.50, AN 7.61, AN 10.3–5, AN 11.3–5

[22] It does not, however, in and of itself confirm the necessity of jhāna for those on the way to stream-entry, since they do not have 'knowledge & vision in accordance with reality'. See SN 25.1. More on these path-attainers below.

as such seems to be one of the unstated factors in such sequences.

54   This passage further clarifies two points in the interpretation of other descriptions of dependent liberation or the path in general. Firstly, samādhi as a crucial support for liberation means right samādhi, which is the four jhānas. When we came across other descriptions of the path that refer to or imply samādhi in less explicit terms, we should therefore infer that jhāna is meant. This is the normal situation in the suttas, since the sequence gladness, rapture, tranquility, bliss, and samādhi elsewhere serves to introduce the four jhānas;[23] sometimes too the divine abidings;[24] or else it develops the spiritual faculties, powers, and enlightenment factors.[25]

55   Secondly, this right samādhi is an essential component of the path, not an optional extra. In contexts such as the gradual training, which include extras such as psychic powers, we must therefore understand that samādhi, no less than virtue or wisdom, cannot be skipped over.

The Seven Purifications

56   The seven purifications shed further light on 'dependent liberation'. They occur only once in the suttas, and once again with two further purifications addended, and are not analyzed in detail. Although of slight importance in the suttas, they were utilized as the framework of the Visuddhimagga, thus assuming great importance for the Theravādin exegetical tradition. Here virtue and samādhi are treated

---

[23] DN 2.25, etc. quoted below.
[24] MN 7.8*ff.* quoted above, MN 40.8.
[25] Vin Mv 8.15 quoted below.

summarily, the focus being on a more detailed breakdown of the stages of insight. This trend continues further in the Paṭisambhidāmagga, and further still in the Visuddhimagga. Perhaps for this reason the seven purifications have played a key role in the attempts to discover a vehicle of 'pure vipassanā' in the suttas. I will endeavor to piece together what the suttas say about these stages. First, the basic statement from the primary source, the Rathavinīta Sutta.

57   'Purification of virtue is for the sake of purification of mind. Purification of mind is for the sake of purification of view. Purification of view is for the sake of purification of overcoming uncertainty. Purification of overcoming uncertainty is for the sake of purification of knowledge & vision of what is and what is not the path. Purification of knowledge & vision of what is and what is not the path is for the sake of purification of knowledge & vision of the way. Purification of knowledge & vision of the way is for the sake of purification of knowledge & vision. Purification of knowledge & vision is for the sake of final Nibbāna without grasping.'[26]

58   The sutta gives the simile of a journey by means of relay carriages. The first carriage takes one as far as the second carriage, but no further. The second carriage takes one as far as the third, but no further. Each carriage has a specific role to play, which cannot be omitted. As usual, the stages are both necessary and helpful conditions, but not sufficient.

59   The individual stages are not defined in the Rathavinīta Sutta, so we must look elsewhere. A related teaching by Venerable Ānanda provides explanations of some factors. The stages of purification are here shown, not as self-sufficient, but as supported by a phalanx of ancillary factors. Though

[26] MN 24.15

wisdom is at work throughout, only after 'purification of mind', which as always is explicitly defined as the four jhānas, does it mature into 'knowledge & vision in accordance with reality'.

60   'And what, Vyagghapajjas, is the factor of striving in the purification of virtue? Here, a monk is virtuous; he trains in the rules of training he has undertaken. This is called purification of virtue. [He thinks:] "I will fulfill such a form of purification when it is unfulfilled, or when it is fulfilled, I will assist it everywhere with understanding." The enthusiasm therein, the effort, the industry, the endeavor, the not holding back, the mindfulness, and the clear comprehension; this is called the factor of striving in the purification of virtue.

61   'And what, Vyagghapajjas, is the factor of striving in the purification of mind? Here, a monk ... enters and abides in the first jhāna... second jhāna... third jhāna... fourth jhāna. This is called purification of mind... The enthusiasm [etc] therein; this is called the factor of striving in the purification of mind.

62   'And what, Vyagghapajjas, is the factor of striving in the purification of view? Here a monk understands in accordance with reality: "This is suffering"..."This is the origin of suffering"..."This is the cessation of suffering"..."This is the way of practice leading to the cessation of suffering." This is called purification of view... The enthusiasm [etc] therein; this is called the factor of striving in the purification of view.

63   'And what, Vyagghapajjas, is the factor of striving in the purification of release? That noble disciple, endowed with the factor of striving in the purification of virtue... of mind... of view, makes lust fade from his mind regarding phenomena provoking lust, and makes his mind release from phenomena which should be released from. Having done so, he contacts right release. This is called purification of release. [He thinks:]

> "I will fulfill such a form of purification when it is un-
> fulfilled, or when it is fulfilled, I will assist it every-
> where with understanding." The enthusiasm therein,
> the effort, the industry, the endeavor, the not holding
> back, the mindfulness, and the clear comprehension;
> this is called the factor of striving in the purification
> of release.'[27]

64   In this sequence, purification of view is the vision of the
four noble truths, which as we noted above, is normally
associated with the stream-enterer.[28] 'Purification of view'
in this group of four occupies the same place where the
seven purifications mention three factors: purification of
view, of overcoming uncertainty, and of knowledge & vision
of what is and what is not the path. These correspond exactly
with the three fetters abandoned by the stream-enterer—
identity view, doubt, and misapprehension of virtue & vows.

65   A possible reading is that these three purifications constitute an expanded explanation of purification of view, de-
tailing the sequence in which these fetters are abandoned
during the course of vipassanā culminating in the vision
of the four noble truths. Having clearly seen what the path
is, the stream-enterer is in a position to perfect their purification of knowledge & vision of the way. This occupies the
equivalent position in this sequence as do 'repulsion' and
'fading away' elsewhere. We noted earlier that these pertain
exclusively to the noble stages; and in the above passage
too, the text changes from 'monk' to 'noble disciple' for the
final purification, the fading away of lust after seeing the
four noble truths.[29] The development of insight culminates

---

[27]   AN 4.194

[28]   Contra Vsm 182

[29]   *Contra* Vsm 21.135

with the purification of knowledge & vision, here surely the knowledge & vision of release pertaining to arahantship.[30]

66 The commentarial notion that these seven stages are completed by the stream-enterer, and that the higher path attainers go around again, each time repeating the sequence of vipassanā knowledges,[31] finds no support in the suttas and contradicts the basic texts and similes, which speak of a one-way, step by step progression. The purpose of developing purification of knowledge & vision is not for the further purification of insight through the higher paths, but for final Nibbana without grasping.

67 Now it is true that in real life things are not so straightforward, and Buddhist causality hinges on these nuances and ramifications. But this does not empower us to simply postulate interpretations without a textual basis. The Rathavinīta sequences is clearly meant to express the primary conditional sequence of practice, to which other elements—supplementary factors, feedback loops, etc.—should be considered as subordinate.

68 This interpretation is somewhat complicated by the nine purifications mentioned in the Dasuttara Sutta, which add purification of understanding and purification of release to the seven.[32] These two extras, occurring only in this late and formalistic sutta, may perhaps be read as an expanded explanation of purification of knowledge & vision.

69 The exact interpretation of the stages of liberating insight, though, does not affect the necessity for jhāna as the purification of mind that precedes all these stages.

[30] *Contra* Vsm 22.1
[31] Vsm 22.22f.
[32] DN 34.22

70   Purification of view can be described from different angles.

71   One monk approached another monk and asked:
        'What does "well-purified vision" refer to?' That monk
        replied: 'When a monk understands in accordance
        with reality the origin and ending of the six bases of
        contact...' Dissatisfied with that explanation, he approached another monk, who said: 'When a monk understands... the five aggregates...' and another monk
        said: 'When a monk understands... the four great elements...' and yet another said: 'When a monk understands in accordance with reality: "Whatever is subject
        to arising, all that is subject to cessation," that is what
        "well-purified vision" refers to.'

72   Dissatisfied with all these answers, that monk approached the Blessed One, who replied: 'Each of those
        true men explained how vision is well purified according to their dispositions, in just the same way that their
        own vision had been well purified.'[33]

73   The Buddha then went on to present the simile of the city
    given above, showing that all of these modes of seeing reality
    are delivered to the mind by samatha and vipassanā.

74   Purification by overcoming uncertainty refers to doubts
    such as: 'Was I in the past? How was I? Will I be in the future?'
    All such speculation is ultimately based on the false notion
    of a permanent self. Seeing the monk Revata the Doubter
    reviewing his purification by overcoming uncertainty, the
    Buddha remarked:

75   'Whatever uncertainties about here or beyond
            One's own or another's feelings [about views]
        The liver of the holy life abandons them all
            Ardently practicing jhāna.'[34]

---

[33] SN 35.245 (condensed)
[34] Ud 5.7; cp. Snp 474. Views are called feelings in DN 1.3.32*ff*.

76   The Buddha's first inspired utterance after his enlightenment describes how he overcame doubt through discernment of conditions. Emerging from seven days' samādhi
absorbed in the 'bliss of liberation', he reflected on dependent origination and spoke the following verses.

77   'When dhammas fully manifest
                To the ardent brahman in jhāna
            Then his doubts all disappear
                Since he understands dhammas and their causes.

78   'When dhammas fully manifest
                To the ardent brahman in jhāna
            Then his doubts all disappear
                Since he has realized the evaporation of conditions.

79   'When dhammas fully manifest
                To the ardent brahman in jhāna
            He stands dispelling Māra's hordes
                Like the sun which lights the sky.'[35]

80   'Knowledge and vision of what is and what is not the path'
seems to occur in only one other passage. In this passage,
the word 'universal' is a technical term for samādhi based
on a perception of an element or color.[36]

81   'This was spoken by the Blessed One in the "Girl's
            Questions":

82   "The attainment of the goal, the peace of the heart;
                Having conquered the army, dear and pleasant seeming,
                Alone, doing jhāna, I awakened to bliss.
            Therefore I make no partners with people—
            Partnership with anyone is not for me."

---

[35] Ud 1.1–3
[36] The Pali is *kasiṇa*, but in the suttas this does not mean 'a disk of color or elements used as a support for preliminary meditation', as described in the Visuddhimagga. See Appendix A for discussion.

83 'Bhante, how should the detailed meaning of this brief statement by the Blessed One be regarded?'

84 'Sister, some contemplatives and brahmans who excell in the attainment of the earth-universal came up with that as the goal. But the extent of excellence in the attainment of the earth-universal was directly known by the Blessed One. Directly knowing thus, he saw the beginning, the danger, the escape, and knowledge & vision of what is and what is not the path. For him, because of seeing these things, the attainment of the goal, the peace of the heart, is known.' [And so on for the other nine universals, concluding with the consciousness-universal.][37]

85 So this knowledge involves developing insight into samādhi based on direct experience. The seven purifications thus involve samādhi, not simply as the precondition for insight at purification of mind, but at each step of the development of insight, specifically including the stages of insight pertaining to stream-entry.

Conclusion

86 In this chapter we have delved into the nature of the conditional relations governing the path of practice. The path embodies the principles of the Dhamma in practical form. The practice and theory of Dhamma can only be provisionally separated; for the sincere practitioner their every moment is a reflection of Dhamma. The serenity they find in their daily life and in their meditation is the experiential proof of the drying up of the flood of defilements. The next chapter shows how these principles find expression in a life of contemplative simplicity.

---

[37] AN 10.26

87   'When the sky pours down rain in big drops on the
mountaintop, the water flows down and fills the mountain cracks and crevices. When the mountain cracks
and crevices are full, they fill the little pools. When the
little pools are full, they fill the great pools. When the
great pools are full, they fill the little rivers. When the
little rivers are full, they fill the great rivers. When the
great rivers are full, they fill the mighty ocean.'[38]

---

[38] SN 12.23

Chapter 5

The Gradual Training

THE GRADUAL TRAINING puts into practice the path described above in abstract. Since it is an example, not a universal principle, there will naturally be some variation when applied to the complexities of the real world. Not everyone will accomplish everything described here; for example, it is not necessary to develop psychic powers. Nevertheless, the prominence of the gradual training and its central role in displaying the detailed workings of the path lend it great authority. Indeed, development of all the key factors of the gradual training is said to be necessary to abandon suffering.[1] The Buddha stresses that each step of the training should be accomplished in order for the practitioner to successfully progress to the next step.[2]

Of all the versions of the gradual training[3] none can rival the Sāmaññaphala Sutta. This very long discourse is the record of a conversation between the Buddha and the newly

---

[1] See e.g. AN 10.76
[2] MN 107.3ff.
[3] MN 27, MN 38, MN 39, MN 51, MN 53, MN 107, MN 125, etc.

crowned King Ajātasattu. This is a truly regal discourse, a literary classic, and a tragedy of mythic proportions. Its power is only enhanced by the fact that the desperate psychological struggle of the king remains in the background, barely hinted at in the discourse. For the sake of concision, unfortunately, we must remain content with an abridgment rather than a full translation. The king, tormented by remorse over a terrible crime, asks the Buddha about happiness.

3   'Bhante, the various craftsmen and workers enjoy here & now the visible fruits of their skills, bringing themselves and their families pleasure and joy, and supporting monks, which leads to happiness in heaven. Is it possible, Bhante, to point out such a fruit of the contemplative life apparent here & now, pertaining to this life?'

4   'It is possible, Great King... Here, a Tathāgata arises in the world, an arahant, a fully enlightened Buddha, perfect in realization and conduct, sublime, knower of the worlds, unexcelled trainer of persons to be tamed, teacher of deities and humans, enlightened, blessed. He makes known this world with its deities, Māras, and Brahmās, this generation with its contemplatives and brahmans, princes and people, having witnessed it himself with direct knowledge. He teaches the Dhamma, beautiful in the beginning, beautiful in the middle, beautiful in the end, meaningful and well phrased, and he elucidates the holy life entirely fulfilled and purified.

5   'A householder hears that Dhamma and gains faith in the Tathāgata. He considers thus: "This household life is cramped and dirty, but life gone forth is wide open. It is not easy while dwelling in a house to live the holy life absolutely fulfilled and purified as a polished shell. What if I were to shave off my hair and beard, put on the dyed robe and go forth from the home to home-

lessness?" And after some time, having abandoned a small or large quantity of wealth, having abandoned a small or large circle of relatives, he goes forth into homelessness.

6   'When he has gone forth he dwells restrained in the role of the monastic code, perfect in conduct and resort, seeing danger in the slightest fault, training in the rules he has undertaken; endowed with good action of body and speech; with purified livelihood; perfect in virtue; with sense doors guarded; endowed with mindfulness and clear comprehension; content.

7   'And how, Great King, is a monk perfect in virtue?

8   'Here a monk has abandoned killing living beings, he has laid down the rod and the sword, and abides compassionate for the welfare of all living beings...

9   'He has abandoned theft, taking only what is given...

10   'He has abandoned what is not the holy life, living remote from the vulgar act of sex...

11   'He has abandoned false speech, speaking what is true and reliable, no deceiver of the world...

12   'He has abandoned divisive speech, delighting and rejoicing in harmony...

13   'He has abandoned harsh speech, speaking what is pleasing to the ear, going to the heart, delightful and pleasing to the manyfolk...

14   'He has abandoned gossip, speaking what is true and meaningful at the right time...

15   'He eats one meal a day...

16   'He refrains from dancing, singing, playing music, and seeing shows...

17   'He refrains from accepting gold and money...

18   'He refrains from storing up food and material possessions...

19   'He refrains from hinting and suggesting, using material goods to gain other material goods...

20   'He refrains from making a living by various trivial sciences such as interpreting omens and dreams, fortune telling, palmistry, astrology, mathematics, worldly poetry and studies, geomancy, and medicine...

21   'And so, Great King, a monk thus perfect in virtue, just like a warrior chief without enemies, does not see fear from any quarter. Endowed with this noble aggregate of virtue he experiences within himself a blameless bliss...

22   'And how, Great King, does a monk guard his sense-doors?

23   'Seeing a form with the eye; hearing a sound with the ear; smelling a smell with the nose; tasting a taste with the tongue; touching a tangible object with the body; and cognizing a phenomena with the mind he does not grasp at general or particular features. Since if he did not restrain his sense faculties he would be overwhelmed by desire and aversion, by evil, unbeneficial qualities, he practices for the restraint and guarding of his sense faculties. Endowed with this noble aggregate of sense restraint, he experiences within himself an unblemished bliss...

24   'And how, Great King, is a monk endowed with mindfulness and clear comprehension?

25   'Here, a monk acts with clear comprehension when going out and returning; when looking in front and to the side; when bending and stretching the limbs; when carrying robes and bowl; when eating and drinking; when urinating and defecating; when walking, standing, sitting, sleeping, waking, speaking, and keeping silent.

26   'And how, Great King, is a monk content?

27   'Here, a monk is content with robes to protect the body and alms-food to sustain the belly. Wherever he goes, he takes just these with him, like a bird which flies, burdened only by its wings...

28   'And so, Great King, endowed with this noble aggregate of virtue, this noble sense restraint, this noble mindfulness and clear comprehension, and this noble contentment he resorts to a secluded dwelling place—a forest, the root of a tree, a mountain, a wilderness, a cave, a charnel ground, a wood, an open space, or a heap of straw. Then after his meal, having returned from alms-round, he sits down cross-legged, sets his body erect, and establishes mindfulness before him.

29   'Having abandoned desire he abides with a mind free from desire. Having abandoned ill will and anger, he is compassionate for the welfare of all living beings. Having abandoned sloth & torpor, he is percipient of light, mindful and clearly comprehending. Having abandoned restlessness & remorse he abides unruffled, with mind inwardly calm. Having abandoned doubt, he is not perplexed regarding beneficial qualities. He purifies his mind from these five hindrances.

30   'When a debtor pays off their debt, or a sick person is cured, or a prisoner is released, or a slave is freed, or a traveler through the desert reaches a safe place, for that reason they would gain gladness and happiness. In just the same way, a monk contemplates these five hindrances when not abandoned in himself as a debt, a sickness, a prison, slavery, a desert journey. He contemplates these five hindrances when they are abandoned in himself as unindebtedness, health, release from prison, freedom, a safe place.

31   'In one who contemplates the abandoning of the five hindrances in oneself, gladness is born. In one who is glad, rapture is born. In one whose mind is rapturous, the body becomes tranquil. One whose body is tranquil feels bliss. The mind of one who is blissful enters samādhi.

32   'Quite secluded from sensual pleasures, secluded from unbeneficial qualities he enters and abides in

the first jhāna. He steeps, soaks, fills, and suffuses his person with rapture and bliss born of seclusion, so that nothing remains unsuffused by rapture and bliss. Just as if an expert bathman were to knead a lump of bath-powder, the entire lump would be soaked with water and yet no water would leak out. In the same way he suffuses his person with rapture and bliss born of seclusion. This, Great King, is a fruit of the contemplative life apparent here & now, pertaining to this life, more exalted and sublime than those described previously.

33   'And again, Great King, a monk enters and abides in the second jhāna. He steeps, soaks, fills, and suffuses his person with rapture and bliss born of samādhi, so that nothing remains unsuffused. Just as if there were a pool of water fed neither by streams nor by rain; but a spring welling up underneath would steep, soak, fill, and suffuse the entire pool with cool water, so that nothing of the pool would remain unsuffused by cool water. In the same way he suffuses his person with rapture and bliss born of samādhi. This too, Great King is a more exalted and sublime fruit of the contemplative life.

34   'And again, Great King, a monk enters and abides in the third jhāna. He steeps, soaks, fills, and suffuses his person with bliss devoid of rapture, so that nothing remains unsuffused. Just as if a lotus were to be born and grow underneath the water without emerging, the entire plant from the roots to the tips would be steeped, soaked, filled and suffused with cool water, so that nothing of the lotus would remain unsuffused by cool water. In the same way he suffuses his person with bliss devoid of rapture. This too, Great King is a more exalted and sublime fruit of the contemplative life.

35   'And again, Great King, a monk enters and abides in the fourth jhāna. He sits having suffused his person with pure bright heart, so that nothing remains unsuffused with pure bright heart. Just as if a man were to sit completely covered, including his head, with white cloth, so that nothing of his person would remain unsuffused by the white cloth, in just the same way he suffuses his person with pure bright heart. This too, Great King, is a more exalted and sublime fruit of the contemplative life.

36   'And so when his mind is thus concentrated in samādhi, is purified, bright, rid of blemishes, free of taints, soft, workable, steady, and attained to imperturbability, he bends and inclines his mind to knowledge & vision. He understands: "This my body is material, made up of the four great elements, produced by mother and father, built up from rice and porridge, subject to impermanence, to rubbing, wearing, breaking up and dispersal; and this my consciousness is caught up and bound up in it." Just as if a man with good sight were to examine a beryl gem in his hand, saying: "This beryl gem is beautiful, well made, clear, and transparent; and through it is strung a blue, yellow, red, white, or brown string." In just the same way he inclines his mind to knowledge & vision. This too, Great King, is a more exalted and sublime fruit of the contemplative life.

37   'And so when his mind is thus concentrated in samādhi, is purified, bright, rid of blemishes, free of taints, soft, workable, steady, and attained to imperturbability, he bends and inclines his mind to creation of a mind-made body... to wielding the various psychic powers... to the divine ear... to knowledge of the minds of others... to recollection of past lives... to the divine eye which sees the passing away and reappearing of beings according to their actions... Each of these is a

fruit of the contemplative life apparent here & now, pertaining to this life, more exalted and sublime than those previously described.

38   'And so when his mind is thus concentrated in samādhi, is purified, bright, rid of blemishes, free of taints, soft, workable, steady, and attained to imperturbability, he bends and inclines his mind to the knowledge of the evaporation of the poisons. He understands in accordance with reality: "This is suffering"... "This is the origin of suffering"... "This is the cessation of suffering"... "This is the way leading to the cessation of suffering"... "These are poisons"... "This is the origin of the poisons"... "This is the cessation of the poisons"... "This is the way leading to the cessation of the poisons." For him knowing & seeing thus, his mind is freed from the poisons of sensual pleasures, existence, and ignorance. When released he knows: "It is released." He understands: "Birth is evaporated; the holy life has been lived; what was to be done has been done; there is no returning to this state of existence."

39   'Just as if, Great King, there were a mountain pool, crystal clear and clean, a man with good sight standing on the bank would see the rocks, pebbles, and shells, and would see the fish swimming about or resting... So too he knows... "There is no returning to this state of existence."

40   'This, Great King, is a fruit of the contemplative life apparent here & now, pertaining to this life, which is more exalted and sublime than those described previously. And, Great King, there is no fruit of the contemplative life more exalted and sublime than this.'[4]

41   King Ajātasattu is an example of the dilemmas of worldly people searching for inner peace. He obviously had great spiritual potential, and respect for those pursuing the path

---

[4]   DN 2

of renunciation. But, goaded on by the evil monk Devadatta, he had murdered his father King Bimbisāra, a stream-
enterer, for the sake of the throne, thus destroying his chance
of seeing the Dhamma. It is because of the inevitable conflict
between worldly ambitions and spiritual aspirations that
the Buddha laid such stress on the way of renunciation.

42 The gradual training is the key paradigm for monastic
practice. Such meticulous care and attention to refinement
of conduct, seclusion, restraint, contentment, and discipline, day in day out, year in year out, provides the optimum
supporting conditions for the refined states of mind that
lead to liberation. So close was the connection between meditation and the life of seclusion in the forest that often they
were virtually equated, as in the Buddha's critique of the
brahmans which follows, so sadly prophetic of the course
Buddhism was to take. There is a pun in the Pali: the word
for scholar (*ajjhāyaka*) also means 'non-jhāna meditator'.

43 'They made leaf huts in the forest and practiced
jhāna in them. They went to the city or village to gather
alms... and then returned to their huts to practice jhāna.
People saw this and noticed how they meditated so
they introduced the title "jhāna meditator" for them...
But some of them, being unable to do jhāna, settled
around towns and villages and composed scriptures.
People saw them doing this and not meditating, so they
introduced the title "scholars" for them... At that time
it was regarded as a low designation, but now it is the
higher.'[5]

44 However, the Buddha never insisted that his followers
must leave the lay life. As in all things, he relied on the maturity of the individual to choose the appropriate course of
action. For those who choose to remain in the household

5 DN 27.23

life, he would point out how to live that life well, to restrain
the defilements, and to incline gradually towards Dhamma.
Whether lay or monastic, practice of the Dhamma is, in its
essence, the same.

45   'There are five things which conduce to the disap-
pearance of the true Dhamma. What five? When monks
and nuns, laymen and laywomen live in disrespect and
are undeferential towards the Buddha... Dhamma...
Sangha... training... samādhi.'[6]

46   The distinction between laypeople and monastics pertains
to moral conduct only; that is, to actions of body and speech.
The world of the mind, though dependent on virtue, lies
beyond it, following natural principles of its own where
distinctions of lifestyle, gender, race, or nationality have
been left behind. Bhikkhunī Somā forcibly makes this point
in her rebuke to Māra's taunt about a woman's 'two-fingered
understanding.'

47   'What does womanhood matter at all
          When the mind is well concentrated in samādhi
          When knowledge flows on steadily
              As one rightly sees Dhamma with vipassanā?

48   'One to whom it might occur
          "I am woman" or "I am man"
          Or "I am anything at all"
              Is fit for Māra to address'[7]

49   The training for the laity will be similar in principles to
the monastic training. In both cases the Buddha urged us to
avoid the 'wrong path'.

50   'Monks, I do not praise wrong practice for either
householders or those gone forth... What is wrong

6   SN 16.13
7   SN 1.523, 524

practice? Wrong view, wrong intention, wrong speech, wrong action, wrong livelihood, wrong effort, wrong mindfulness, wrong samādhi.'[8]

51   While the Buddha emphasized the basics of generosity, faith, and virtue for laypeople, he encouraged them to go further than that and, like the monastics, to strive to develop the bliss of meditation.

52   'Householder, you have supplied robes, alms-food, dwellings, and medicines for the Sangha of monks, yet you should not be content with just that much. Therefore you should train yourself: "Come now, from time to time I should enter & abide in the rapture of seclusion." '[9]

53   While in conventional Buddhism the lay community is typically encouraged to practice of generosity and virtue, it is often forgotten that these good practices yield their highest benefit when they lead to deep meditation. In the following passage, the wise lady Visākhā explains to the Buddha why she has asked for the privilege of supplying the Sangha in Sāvatthī with eight specific kinds of requisites.

54   'Bhante, monks will come to Sāvatthī when the rains retreat is completed in order to see the Blessed One. They will approach the Blessed One and ask: "Bhante, a monk called such and such has passed away — what is his destiny, his future course?" The Blessed One will explain that as the fruit of stream-entry, once-return, non-return, or arahantship. I will approach them and ask: "Bhante, did that venerable one ever come to Sā-vatthī?" If they say "Yes, he did", then I will come to the conclusion that surely that venerable one used a rains cloth, or food for those arriving or leaving, or food for

8   SN 45.24
9   AN 5.176

the sick or those attending the sick, or medicine for the sick, or porridge. Recollecting that, gladness will be born in me. Being glad, rapture will be born in me. Being rapturous, my body will become tranquil. Being of tranquil body, I will feel bliss. Being blissful, my mind will enter samādhi. That will develop the spiritual faculties, spiritual powers, and enlightenment factors in me. Seeing this benefit, Bhante, I ask the Tathāgata for these eight favors.'

'Sadhu! Sadhu! Visākhā. It is good that seeing this benefit you ask the Tathāgata for these eight favors. I allow you, Visākhā, these eight favors.'[10]

In modern times, vipassanā teachers often say that the deep stillness of samatha meditation is not suitable for lay practitioners. However, although lay people practiced satipaṭṭhāna 'from time to time',[11] it was never singled out as being particularly appropriate for them. The Satipaṭṭhāna Saṁyutta records satipaṭṭhāna being taught to lay people on only two occasions—both times to non-returners on their deathbeds.[12] More typically, lay meditators were encouraged to develop the divine abidings or the six recollections.

The Buddha never taught lay meditation retreats or established any lay meditation centers. The intensive retreat seems to have been for monastics only. This is quite in tune with the gradual training, which sees higher states of mind emerging, not from strenuous toil for a short time in artificial conditions divorced from everyday life, but from a holistic lifestyle of simplicity, contentment, and restraint. This distinguishing feature of the Buddha's dispensation

---

[10] Vin Mv 8.15
[11] MN 51.4
[12] SN 47.29, SN 47.30

was one of the 'monuments to the Dhamma' proclaimed by King Pasenadi.

58 'Bhante, I see some contemplatives and brahmans leading a limited holy life for ten, twenty, thirty, or forty years, and then on a later occasion I see them well groomed and well anointed, with trimmed hair and beards, enjoying themselves provided and endowed with the five cords of sensual pleasure. But here I see monks leading the perfect and pure holy life as long as life and breath last.'[13]

59 In Theravāda meditation retreats, meditators will typically undertake the mildly ascetic vows of the eight precepts while on retreat, which includes no food after midday. Skipping the evening meal is for some a grueling asceticism; but for others it's a chance to lose weight. Here's the Buddha's droll assessment of the benefits of intermittent starvation.

60 '[Some contemplatives] take food once a day... or once a week... or once a fortnight; they dwell pursuing the practice of taking food at stated intervals.'

61 'But do they survive on so little, Aggivessana?'

62 'No, Master Gotama. Sometimes they consume various sorts of delicious food, delicacies, and drinks. That way they regain their strength, fortify themselves, and become fat.'

63 'What they earlier abandoned, Aggivessana, they later gather together again. That is how there is increase and decrease of this body.'[14]

64 Rather than plunging in at the deep end of spiritual life at a meditation intensive, lay people were encouraged to spend one day a week in the monastery, keeping eight pre-

---

[13] MN 89.10
[14] MN 36.5

cepts, listening to Dhamma, and practicing meditation. This practice is continued in some places today.

65   'Now do you Sakyans keep the observance day endowed with eight precepts?'

66   'Well, sometimes we do, Bhante, and sometimes we don't.'

67   'It is no gain for you Sakyans, it is ill-gained that in this life with its fear of sorrow, fear of death, sometimes you keep the observance day and sometimes you don't. What do you think, Sakyans?... What if a man day in, day out were to earn a hundred dollars, a thousand dollars and were to invest his earnings throughout his life of a hundred years, would he not achieve a great mass of wealth?'

68   'Yes, Bhante.'

69   'Well, would that man because of his wealth, owing to his wealth, abide exclusively experiencing bliss for one day and night? Or for half a day and night?'

70   'No, Bhante. For what reason? Sensual pleasures, Bhante, are impermanent, hollow, false, delusory.'

71   'Here, Sakyans, one of my disciples abiding diligent, ardent, and resolute, practicing according to my instructions... for one day and night would abide exclusively experiencing bliss for a hundred years, a hundred times a hundred years, a hundred times a thousand years, a hundred times a hundred thousand years. And he would be a once-returner, a non-returner, or without question a stream-enterer. It is no gain for you, Sakyans, it is ill-gained that in this life with its fear of sorrow, fear of death, sometimes you keep the observance day and sometimes you don't.'

72   'From this day on, Bhante, we will keep the observance day endowed with eight precepts.'[15]

---

[15] AN 10.46

73   Some lay disciples were skilled in the highest reaches of meditation. The following sutta records the time that the Sangha arrived in the village of Veḷukaṇṭaka, where one of the local lay followers was Uttarā Nandamātā, the foremost female devotee in jhāna practice. She was ready waiting to offer the travelling monks food. Venerable Sāriputta asked her how she knew in advance of the Sangha's arrival. That morning, it seems, a passing deity had stopped to hear her chanting.

74   'Having arisen in the night before dawn, Bhante, and chanted the "Way to the Beyond,"[16] I was silent. Then Great King Vessavaṇa, realizing that I had finished reciting, congratulated me: "Sadhu, sister! Sadhu, sister!"

75   '"But who is this of majestic countenance?"

76   '"I, sister, am your brother, Great King Vessavaṇa."[17]

77   '"Sadhu, Your Majesty! May this passage of Dhamma which I have chanted be my gift to you."

78   '"Sadhu, sister! Then let this be a gift for me: tomorrow the Sangha of monks headed by Sāriputta and Moggallāna will arrive here at Veḷukaṇṭaka without having eaten. Having fed the Sangha of monks may you dedicate the offering to me, then that will be a gift for me."

79   'So let the merit of this offering be for the happiness of Great King Vessavaṇa.'

80   'It is wonderful, Nandamātā, it is marvelous that you should converse face to face with Great King Vessavaṇa, a deity of such great psychic power and potency!'

81   'This is not my only wonderful and marvelous quality, Bhante... When rulers for some reason took my

---

[16] Snp 1032-1123. The 'Vatthugāthā' in its current form is no doubt later.
[17] Vessavaṇa was stream-enterer, and so he was Uttarā's Dhamma brother.

dear beloved son by force and killed him... I know of no change in my mind...

82
    'When my husband, who had passed away and re-arisen in a spirit world, revealed himself to me in his old form, I know of no change in my mind on that account...

83
    'Since I was a maiden brought to my youthful husband, I've never betrayed him in thought, how then in body?...

84
    'Since I declared myself a lay devotee, I know of no deliberate violation of any training rule...

85
    'As far as I wish, I enter and abide in the first jhāna... second jhāna... third jhāna... fourth jhāna...

86
    'I do not see any of the five lower fetters taught by the Blessed One unabandoned in me...'

87
    'Wonderful, Nandamātā! Marvelous, Nandamātā!'[18]

88
Such advanced lay disciples attained those levels by following a comprehensive daily training as similar to the monastic path as possible. The Buddha asks Ānanda to speak on this.

89
    'Ānanda, clarify the practice of a trainee for the Sakyans of Kapilavatthu...'

90
    'Here, a noble disciple is virtuous, guards his sense faculties, is moderate in eating, and devoted to wakefulness. He possesses seven good qualities (faith, conscience, fear of wrong-doing, learning, energy, mindfulness, and understanding) and he attains at will, without trouble or difficulty, the four jhānas which constitute the higher mind and are a blissful abiding here & now...'[19]

91
Some say that times have changed and it is no longer possible to find the quiet and solitude necessary for deep samā-

---

[18] AN 7.50
[19] MN 53.6

dhi. There is some truth to this, with the loss of most of the forests and the pervasion of technology and noise pollution. But it's always been hard, and that shouldn't stop us from trying. Even today there are tens of thousands of Buddhist monks, nuns, and lay people who live constantly or for extended periods in peaceful and secluded places suitable for meditation. Most of these places, right now, have empty rooms or empty huts ready for anyone who wants to practice.

92 'Live enjoying retreat, monks, live delighting in retreat, developing samatha of the heart within, not neglecting jhāna, possessing vipassanā, and frequenting empty places. If you do so, one of two fruits may be expected—profound knowledge here & now or, there still being some residual defilement, the state of non-returning.'[20]

---

[20] Iti 2.45

Chapter 6

The Benefits of Samādhi

'A monk who develops and makes much of the four jhānas slopes, flows, and inclines towards Nibbana.'

— THE BUDDHA, SN 53.1

WHY IS THIS SO? The Buddha often praised the jhānas as 'blissful abidings here & now'. Does this imply that jhānas are just escapism, a refined form of solitary vice? Why are jhānas blissful? To understand this, we must first consider the nature of pleasure. The Buddha made a clear distinction between the sensuality that is regarded as pleasure in the world, and the peace of mind that he himself saw as the source of true happiness.

Sensuality

2   'There are these five cords of sensual pleasures. What five? Visible forms cognizable by the eye... sounds cognizable by the ear... smells cognizable by the nose... tastes cognizable by the tongue... tangibles cognizable

by the body that are wished for, desired, alluring, likable, connected with sensual pleasure, and provocative of lust."[1]

3   'Suppose, Aggivessana, there were a high mountain not far from a village or town, and two friends would leave the village or town and approach the mountain hand in hand. Having reached it, one friend would remain below at the foot of the mountain while the other would climb to the top. Then the friend who remained below at the foot of the mountain would say to the friend who stood on the top: "Well, friend, what do you see, standing on top of the mountain?" And the other replied: "I see lovely parks, groves, meadows, and ponds." Then the first friend would say: "It's impossible, friend, it cannot happen that while standing on top of the mountain you should see lovely parks, groves, meadows, and ponds."

4   'Then the other friend would come down to the foot of the mountain, take his friend by the arm, and make him climb to the top of the mountain. After giving him a few moments to catch his breath, he would ask: "Well, friend, standing on top of the mountain, what do you see?" And he would reply: "Standing on top of the mountain, friend, I see lovely parks, groves, meadows, and ponds." Then the other would say: "Friend, just a little earlier we heard you say: 'It is impossible, friend, it cannot happen that while standing on top of the mountain you should see lovely parks, groves, meadows, and ponds.' But now we heard you say [just the opposite]." Then the first friend would reply: "Because I was obstructed by this high mountain, friend, I did not see what was there to be seen."

5   'So too, Aggivessana, Prince Jayasena is obstructed, hindered, blocked, and enveloped by a still greater mass than this—the mass of ignorance. Thus it is im-

---

[1]   MN 13.7 etc.

possible that Prince Jayasena, living in the midst of
sensual pleasures, enjoying sensual pleasures, being
devoured by thoughts of sensual pleasures, being con-
sumed by the fever of sensual pleasures, bent on the
search for sensual pleasures, could know, see, or witness that which must be known through renunciation,
seen through renunciation, attained through renunciation, witnessed through renunciation.'[2]

6   'I have never seen or heard of a king or a king's min-
ister in the past, future, or present, enjoying themselves with the five cords of sensual pleasure, who
without abandoning craving & fever for sensual pleasures, was able to abide with mind... at peace within
himself.

7   'On the contrary, Māgandiya, those contemplatives
and brahmans in the past, future, or present, who
abide with a mind at peace within themselves, all do
so having understood in accordance with reality the
origin, ending, gratification, danger, and escape from
sensual pleasures, and having abandoned craving &
fever for sensual pleasures.'[3]

8   'Where sensual pleasures end and those who have
thoroughly ended sensual pleasures abide, certainly
those venerables are wishless and quenched, crossed
over and gone beyond with respect to that factor, I
say. Where do sensual pleasures end and those who
have thoroughly ended sensual pleasures abide? Who-
ever should say: "I do not know or see that" should
be told: "Here, friend, a monk, quite secluded from
sensual pleasures, secluded from unbeneficial qualities, enters and abides in the first jhāna... Here sensual
pleasures end and those who have thoroughly ended
sensual pleasures abide." Certainly, monks, the guile-

---

[2] MN 125.9

[3] MN 75.17–18

less and undeceitful person would exclaim "Sadhu!"
and rejoice and admire what was said, revering and
honoring the speaker with palms joined in homage.'[4]

9   Sensual desire is not restricted to sexual desire, or desire for food, etc. These are only the overt symptoms of the
hunger for stimulation which constantly obsesses the minds
of beings. Any interest or concern whatsoever connected
with experiencing pleasure, relief, or comfort through the
eye, ear, nose, tongue, or body, or any thoughts, memories,
or expectations of such experience fall within the range of
this prime hindrance. This is the defining characteristic of
beings in the 'sensual world' and the chief reason for taking
rebirth in this realm. Having taken rebirth here, life is for
the most part dedicated to maximizing the experience of
sensual pleasure. Hardly a few seconds ever go by during the
course of an entire life truly free from harassment by concern for sensual pleasure. Even the overwhelming majority
of religious practitioners—and here Buddhists are no exception—are motivated largely by sensual desire, whether
it be the desire to experience refined sensual objects in a
heavenly realm, or the desire to enjoy one's relationships
and material comforts with mind at peace.

10   The pleasure of sensuality is narrow, occurring in only a
restricted zone of the totality of awareness, thus forcing a
constriction of consciousness. It is evanescent, necessitating
a constant toil to seek out new pleasures. It is stimulating,
agitating the mind so that it cannot experience the pleasure
fully, but keeps restlessly skipping about, thus concealing
the inadequacy of the gratification provided by the pleasure.
It is crude, coarsening the mind and blocking awareness of
subtle realities. It is always interwoven with painful feeling,

---

[4]   AN 9.33

pressuring the mind to reject or deny part of experience. It is selfish, obstructing relationships with others based on genuine compassion and altruism. And because of all these things, it promotes the growth of unwholesome thoughts and intentions, leading to suffering in future lives and obstructing the path to Nibbana.

11   The bliss of the peaceful mind shares none of these faults. It permeates the whole field of awareness, so that the mind is spacious and relaxed. Though of course impermanent, it is far more stable and enduring than sensual happiness. It is peaceful, soothing the fevered mind, drawing the mind into the stillness of deep, sustained contemplation. It is of surpassing subtlety, the limits of feeling, pointing the way to the transcendence of feeling. It is pure bliss without any admixture of pain, fostering a truly holistic awareness. It removes any motivation for relationships based on selfish desires; seeing the tenderness of one's own heart, one would shrink away from any act which would harm the heart of another. And because of all these things, it is exclusively associated with wholesome thoughts and intentions, leading to bliss not only in this life, but also to unimaginable ages of bliss in the future. It is the high road to the ultimate bliss of Nibbana.

12   Shortly before his Awakening, the Buddha, having reached the extreme of pain through self-mortification, reflected on the experience of jhāna he had as a child, and asked himself the crucial question:

13   'Why am I afraid of that bliss which has nothing to do with sensual pleasures and unbeneficial qualities? It occurred to me: "I am not afraid of that bliss,

since it has nothing to do with sensual pleasures and unbeneficial qualities."'[5]

Perception

14   According to fundamental principles of Buddhist philosophy, it is the mind which creates the world. The mind, fueled with craving and attachments, cooks up the five senses to feed, distract, and entertain it, to avoid at any cost the ghastly possibility of having to confront the grisly reality behind its cozy complacency. By assailing the mind with an overload of input, the five hindrances, hand in hand with the five senses, confuse and sully the ability to clearly know.

15   'Ignorance has a nutriment, I say. And what is the nutriment of ignorance?

16   '"The five hindrances" should be the reply.'[6]

17   The importance of this statement can scarcely be overstated. It echoes the fundamental truth that one in samādhi knows & sees according to reality the four noble truths. The practice of jhāna, by cutting off the five hindrances, starves ignorance of its food. But how exactly does samādhi accomplish this?

18   One of the key factors in meditation is perception (saññā). Perception is a relatively shallow mode of knowing which recognizes the surface features of phenomena, interpreting them in terms of past experience. It marks off one section of sense data so that it can be treated as a unit. For example, it is perception that generalizes and summarizes the data in a visual image, recognizing that 'This is blue, this is yellow,

---

[5]   MN 36.32
[6]   AN 10.61

this is red.' It filters, simplifies, and abstracts the sheer bewildering quantity of sense data, processing it in terms of manageable information, symbols, and labels. Perception forms the basis of concepts. While perception recognizes common features of phenomena, concepts combine a group or class of features into a mental image or idea. In order to construct something as ephemeral as a concept, the mind must be actively diverted from the clamor of sense experience and applied inwards.

19   The formation of a concept can be analyzed in two stages. First there is the initial conception of a verbal idea, a thought (*vitakka*). Secondly, a sustained series of these thoughts is linked up to form a coherent consideration (*vicāra*). At this stage, this thinking and considering is still preoccupied with perceptions of sense experience; but the mind is able for the first time to be aware of a mental object distinct from that experience, and hence by reflection to infer the existence of a 'mind' as experiencer. This development, though crucial for both psychology and philosophy, introduces a subtle distortion in experience. By representing the world as more coherent and meaningful than it really is, it invites an insidious obsession with the fantasy realm of concepts, the fairy castles of the imagination, divorced from the uncertainties of reality. This process is described with uncanny precision in this famous passage from the Madhupiṇḍika Sutta.

20   'Dependent on the eye and visible forms arises eye-consciousness. The coming together of the three is contact. Due to contact there is feeling. What one feels, one perceives. What one perceives, one thinks about. What one thinks about, one proliferates about. What one proliferates about is the source from which ideas derived from the proliferation of perceptions beset

a person regarding past, future, and present visible
forms cognizable by the eye [and so on].'[7]

21   The first steps of this passage repeat the basic exposition
of how consciousness works as analyzed in dependent origination. Our primary sense experience is the 'given', the raw
materials common to all sentient beings.

22   As this sense experience stimulates a response of liking,
disliking, or disinterest, however, these feelings move towards a more active response to sense stimuli, which our
passage reflects with a new syntactical structure. The static
nouns are replaced by verbs—the momentum is picking up.
The mind is adding to experience, and here perception plays
a key role, under the influence of the four 'perversions of
perception'—seeing permanence in what is impermanent,
happiness in what is suffering, self in what is not-self, and
beauty in what is ugly.[8] Perception notices shared charac-
teristics, so that each experience suggests an association
with further phenomena. These associations become verbal-
ized internally as mental images called 'thinking'. Thinking
then expands and gets out of control in 'proliferation' (*pa-
pañca*). The following verse links 'proliferation' closely with
'conceit', the idea of a 'self'.

23   'One should thoroughly dig up the root
                Of the proliferating concept
                 "I am the thinker." '[9]

24   'Proliferation' is the way the undisciplined mind, by identifying with and delighting in this process of thinking, erupts
in a profusion of trivial and repetitious inner commentaries.

---

[7]   MN 18.16. The subtle dynamics of this passage were explored by
      Bhikkhu Ñāṇānanda in his classic study *Concept and Reality*.
[8]   AN 4.49
[9]   Snp 916

So at this point the passage moves on from analysis purely in terms of mental factors—the 'person' is introduced. Proliferation has given birth to the full-blown concept of a 'thinker' who is being overwhelmed by the conceptual process by which they were born, which is now spinning out of control.

25   Significantly, at the same point time is introduced. The 'person' is precisely that stable, unchanging entity that is assumed to persist through the past, present, and future.

26   The 'ideas' spoken of in the passage lie close in meaning to 'concepts'; but the literal meaning 'reckonings, classifications' suggests rather more specifically the mind's calculating manipulation of the data of experience, like an inner spin doctor reaffirming the self and its place in the world.

27   The point of this passage is to show how uncontrolled proliferation is not merely the source of anxiety, confusion, or emotional upset, but is integral to the very origination of suffering. Since this is the case, the benefits of a meditation which can quell thought are not restricted to short term psychological ease. We have met such a meditation before.

28   'Mindfulness of breathing should be developed in order to cut off thinking.'[10]

29   It was seen above how perception simplifies experience into meaningful units. This essential function is undermined when proliferative thinking re-multiplies experience, so that just one word can trigger minutes or hours of discursive inner monologue. The special quality of mindfulness of breathing, shared to some degree with other meditation subjects, is to cut this process before it sprouts by staying with singleness of perception. When disciplined through

---

[10] Ud 4.1, etc.

meditation, the simplifying function of perception radically reduces the quantity of data in experience, allowing the development of a more refined and sensitive awareness.

30   If we are to understand this process a little better, we should start be reflecting on what exactly the 'breath' is. There is a certain experience at the beginning of each breath, a different experience in the middle, and yet another at the end. These experiences are simply awareness of the air element; but it is perception that marks them off as the 'breath'. Only the physical impact of the air on the nerve endings is registered by body consciousness. That body consciousness 'reports' to mind consciousness, which performs the more sophisticated cognitive tasks such as recognition, interpretation, and so on.

31   The function of *vitakka* to initiate thoughts and *vicāra* to sustain chains of thoughts is transformed by applying them not to perceptions of verbal constructs but to perceptions of the breath, actively directing the mind away from the diversity of sense experience onto the breath. Doing so over and over, the common features of the breaths become apparent. By combining the shared features of the breaths recognized by perception and by ignoring irrelevant data, the mind forms a stable and coherent concept or mental image of the breath.

32   As contemplation deepens, the physical breath becomes very fine, so that its impact, originally overpowering, fades and the settling mind gains more appreciation of the subtle mind consciousness. Here, the meditator is going beyond the first four steps of mindfulness of breathing which fall within body contemplation.

33   A numinous rapture arises; the mind floats up like a balloon relieved of its ballast as the heavy burden of the body

is disappearing. The subtle reflection of the mind in the breath is now almost the sole object in awareness. This refined concept, because of ignoring fluctuations in detail, has an enduring quality which outlives the changing physical phenomena it is derived from, in just the same way than the concept of 'self' has an enduring quality which outlives the body.[11] It normally appears to the meditator as a brilliant light of awesome power, yet exquisite refinement.

34   As the fluctuations in consciousness even out, change fades away. One need no longer rely on memories of past experiences to interpret the present moment. The contrast on which time depends is not evident, and past and future disappear in the seamless flow of the present: onepointedness in time. The contents of experience become so rarefied that signs and summaries are rendered superfluous. A deeper mode of knowing emerges.

35   'Quite secluded from sensual pleasures, secluded from unbeneficial qualities one enters and abides in the first jhāna... One's former perception of sensual pleasures ceases. On that occasion there is a subtle & true perception of rapture & bliss born of seclusion. Thus with training some perceptions arise and some perceptions cease... Again, one enters and abides in the second jhāna... third jhāna... fourth jhāna... base of infinite space... base of infinite consciousness... base of nothingness. One's former perception of the base of infinite consciousness ceases. On that occasion there is a subtle & true perception of the base of nothingness... Thus with training, some perceptions arise and some perceptions cease.

36   Potthapāda, from when a monk gains his own [inner] perception, he then step by step gradually con-

---

[11] This does not, however, imply that concepts are not classified as conditioned and impermanent, as some suggest. See SN 15.20.

tacts the peak of perception. Standing on the peak of perception it occurs to him: "Volition is evil to me; non-volition is better. If I were to form volitions and acts of will, this perception of mine would cease, and another, coarser, perception would arise. What if I were to neither form volitions nor acts of will?" ... Those perceptions cease and other, coarser, perceptions do not arise. He contacts cessation.

37   Thus, Poṭṭhapāda, there is the gradual attainment of the cessation of higher perceptions with clear comprehension."[12]

Knowledge

38   If one is disinterested in these five senses and withdraws attention from them, how would they continue to exist? This is a simple matter, one that we can observe everyday in our ordinary acts of inattention. What we are not interested in, we turn away from, and it vanishes from our field of awareness. This happens to all of us every minute of every day, and in samādhi this ordinary feature of the mind is developed to a whole new level—as with so many things in samādhi.

39   The five senses disappear, together with their associated feelings, perceptions, thoughts, memories, intentions, and consciousnesses. When they stop, there is the first experiential understanding of 'cessation' at a really deep level. This is why the whole path of practice is called a 'gradual cessation'. And cessation can be a terrifying thing. For one who lacks grounding in this experience, the dawning realization of the frailty and emptiness of all one holds dear can precipitate a traumatic existential crisis.

---

[12] DN 9.10–17

40   'Here, monk, some have such a view: "This is the self, this is the world. After death I will be permanent, everlasting, eternal, not subject to change, and will remain just like eternity." He hears the Tathāgata or a disciple of the Tathāgata teaching Dhamma for the destruction of all standpoints for views, resolutions, obsessions, insistings, and inherent compulsions, for the relinquishing of all belongings, for the evaporation of craving, for fading away, cessation, Nibbana. It occurs to him: "Good grief! I shall be annihilated! Good grief! I shall perish! Good grief! I shall not exist!" He sorrows, grieves, and laments, beats his breast, and becomes distraught. Thus there is anxiety about what is non-existent within.'[13]

41   The question then is, how do we cope with this? How do we prepare our mind, little by little, to accept emptiness? Once again, this is where jhāna comes in. Jhānas share, to a lesser degree, the bliss of cessation which is Nibbana. In fact, jhānas are called, with qualification, 'deathless', 'Nibbana here & now', 'Nibbana', even 'final Nibbana'.[14] The gradual abiding in jhāna, witnessing the successive stilling of activities, prepares the mind to accept that Nibbana is ultimate bliss, precisely because all feelings have ended.

42   Venerable Sāriputta addressed the monks: 'Nibbana is bliss, friends, Nibbana is bliss.'

43   When this was said, Venerable Udāyin said to Venerable Sāriputta: 'But what is the bliss there, in that nothing is felt?'

44   'Just that is the bliss there, in that nothing is felt... The bliss & happiness that arise dependent on the five cords of sensual pleasure; this is called the bliss of sensual pleasure. Here, a monk, quite secluded from

---

[13] MN 22.20
[14] AN 9.48*ff.*

> sensual pleasures, secluded from unbeneficial quali-
> ties, enters and abides in the first jhāna... If perception
> and attention connected with sensual pleasure assail
> one abiding thus, this is an affliction for him, just as
> if pain arises in a happy person. Affliction has been
> called suffering by the Blessed One. By this method it
> should be understood how Nibbana is bliss...'[15]

45　Once the mind has experienced jhāna, it will deeply understand the suffering of sense-activity and will be reluctant
to get involved, remaining free from defilements for a long
time. It can then engage in contemplation of Dhamma without being diverted by distracting thoughts, sleepiness, or
desire, and can pursue any theme of meditation as long as
it wishes.

46　　　　'When the mind is released from these five taints
> [hindrances], it is soft, workable, radiant, not brittle,
> it has right samādhi for the evaporation of the poisons.
> One can incline the mind to witness with direct knowl-
> edge any principle which can be witnessed with direct
> knowledge, and become an eyewitness in every case,
> there being a suitable basis.'[16]

47　These direct knowledges have been met with above in the
examination of satipaṭṭhāna and the gradual training. Although not absolutely necessary, their frequent occurrence
in the suttas indicates that they should not be dismissed
lightly. They include such important psychic powers as the
ability to recollect one's past lives and to see how beings are
reborn according to their actions. These confirm through
personal experience the truth of action and rebirth, which
constitutes ordinary right view. This will ripen into the transcendental right view of the four noble truths—how the

---

[15]　AN 9.34
[16]　AN 5.23; cp. SN 46.33.

process of rebirth works and how to bring it to an end. These are distinct kinds of knowledge; but the clearer is the knowledge of the details of rebirth, the easier will be the understanding of the principles of rebirth. The practice of jhāna will naturally lead to this kind of understanding by demonstrating how the mind can exist quite happily when relieved of the burden of the body. It is no coincidence that reports of near-death experiences—being drawn down a tunnel of light, meeting heavenly beings, feeling great bliss—are so similar to experiences commonly met with on the threshold of jhāna. To get into jhāna, one has to die to the body.

48   I noted above how the ability of the mind to form concepts is the basis of both the idea of 'self' and the attainment of jhāna. As the unseen seer, the 'lord of the city in the center at the crossroads', the mind is the prime resort of the 'self'. Mind consciousness plays a role in the processing of all the other kinds of consciousness, and therefore can easily be mistaken for a permanent substratum of experience. Further, as it is within the mind that the idea of 'self' is born, when the mind is seeking for some aspect of experience to appropriate as 'self', it is automatically prone to turn back in on itself rather than seek outside. So we have seen that freedom from attachment to the mind is the exclusive province of the noble ones. For those who start practice with wrong views, then, the mind in jhāna becomes the obvious locus for theories of the self. But one who starts practice with right view will instead use their jhāna as a basis for insight into the nature of awareness.

49   Jhānas are 'the end of the world'.[17] Five coarse kinds of consciousness have disappeared, leaving only the purified mind consciousness. Here, consciousness is directly acces-

---

[17] AN 9.38

sible to profound contemplation. Not catching a glimpse of it here and there like a butterfly flitting in the twilight gloom of the forest, but gazing at it face to face for a long time, like a butterfly that has come to rest on one's hand in the clear light of day. Before, the 'self' could always shift its ground when challenged. But now it has been tracked to its last stronghold: consciousness itself. But why so many words?

50   'There are these four ways of devotion to the pursuit of pleasure, Cunda, which conduce exclusively to repulsion, fading away, cessation, peace, direct knowledge, enlightenment, Nibbana. What four? Here, a monk... enters and abides in the first jhāna... second jhāna... third jhāna... fourth jhāna.

51   'If wanderers from other religions should say: "The monks who are sons of the Sakyan abide devoted to these four ways of pursuing pleasure", they should be told: "Yes!" since they speak rightly, without misrepresenting the truth.

52   'If wanderers from other religions should ask: "How many fruits and benefits are there from devotion to these four ways of pursuing pleasure?" They should be told: "There are four fruits, four benefits. What four? Here, a monk... becomes a stream-enterer... a once-returner... a non-returner... an arahant." '[18]

---

[18] DN 29.24

Chapter 7

Jhāna & the Noble Ones

'The four who are on the way
And the four established in the fruit—
This is the Sangha upright
With understanding, virtue, and samādhi.'

— THE BUDDHA, SN 1.916

ALL THE EXPOSITIONS OF THE PATH include samādhi
as a central element. This being so, we should expect that
samādhi will be one of the intrinsic qualities ascribed to the
noble individuals, those who bring the path to life.

According to Buddhism, the path to Awakening is divided
into four stages, each of which is further subdivided into
the 'way to' and the 'realization of' each stage. These eight
kinds of enlightened individual are referred to in many different ways in the suttas: 'noble one' (*ariya*), 'true person'
(*sappurisa*), 'trainee' (*sekha*), and so on.

In this chapter the key sutta statements about the samādhi of the noble ones are collected, starting with the fully

accomplished arahant and working down to those who have barely entered the path. In the passage below, the phrase 'noble one' refers to the arahant, not to those at all stages of Awakening, as normal.

4   'Monks, there are ten ways of noble living, by which noble ones have dwelt in the past, will dwell in the future, and are dwelling now. What ten?

5   'Here, monks, a monk has abandoned the five hindrances; has equanimity towards the six senses; guards mindfulness; is supported by using, enduring, avoiding, or dispelling after reflection; has rejected personal speculations about the truth; has utterly dismissed all searching; has unclouded intention; having tranquilized the bodily activity [of the breath]... he enters and abides in the fourth jhāna; has mind well released with the abandoning of lust, anger, and delusion; and has understanding well released by understanding that lust, anger, and delusion have been permanently uprooted. Whatever noble ones that lived in the past, will live in the future, or are living now, all of them live according to these ten ways of noble living.'[1]

6   Elsewhere, the first jhāna is shown to be the minimum necessary prerequisite for arahantship;[2] but this sutta confirms that all arahants would have access to fourth jhāna after their attainment. Notice that with this fourth jhāna the breath is tranquillized. This must be a gradual process of settling, occurring at the very least over several minutes, and so ruling out any 'momentary' or transcendental 'pathmoment' samādhi.

7   For the arahant, free from all defilements, there is nothing to prevent the attainment of jhāna.

---

[1]   AN 10.20 condensed.
[2]   E.g. MN 64, AN 9.36.

8   'Monk, having abandoned six things one can enter
and abide in the first jhāna. What six? Sensual desire,
ill will, sloth & torpor, restlessness & remorse, doubt;
and the danger in sensual pleasures has been well seen
with right understanding in accordance with reality.'[3]

9   To hold that an arahant may not attain jhāna is therefore
tantamount to implying that they may still be subject to
residual defilements.

10   The historical context here is revealing. In virtually all
other schools of Buddhism, a threefold development occurred contemporaneous with the development of the jhāna-
less arahant in the Theravāda. Firstly, the Buddha was exalted from being a perfected human to being a god; secondly,
the arahant was downgraded, subject, it was felt, to residual
sensuality, lack of universal knowledge, even selfishness;
and thirdly, the Bodhisattva ideal emerged from obscurity
to fill the resulting gap as an alternative way of practice.
These trends culminated in the Mahāyāna. In an attenuated
form, the first and third of these trends are also evident in
the Theravāda commentaries. So it is no surprise that the
status of the arahant is gradually eroded.

11   Some scholars, however, derive the jhāna-less arahant
from one described in the suttas as 'released by understanding'. This is, however, not how the 'one released from understanding' is described in the suttas.

12   '"Released by understanding, released by understanding", is said, friend. What was the Blessed One
referring to when he spoke of the one released by understanding?'

13   'Here, friend, a monk... enters and abides in the first
jhāna. He understands that. This is what the Blessed

---

[3]   AN 6.73

One was referring to, with qualification, when he spoke
of the one released by understanding. Again... he enters and abides in the second jhāna... third jhāna...
fourth jhāna... base of infinite space... base of infinite
consciousness... base of nothingness... base of neither
perception nor non-perception... cessation of perception and feeling. Having seen with understanding, his
poisons are completely evaporated. He understands
that. This is what the Blessed One was referring to,
without qualification, when he spoke of the one released by understanding.'[4]

14   Elsewhere, however, the arahant released by understanding is, somewhat inconsistently, said to not dwell in the formless attainments.[5] The main point, then, is not which level
of samādhi is achieved, but the emphasis on wisdom at each
level. Nowhere in the suttas is it stated or implied that an
arahant released by understanding does not attain the four
jhānas.

15   It is clear enough, then, that all arahants must, according
to the emphatic and clear statements of the suttas, possess
jhāna. What, then, of the next lower grade of noble one,
the non-returner (*anāgāmi*)? The non-returner shares with
the arahant the distinction of being 'perfected in samādhi'.
With a typically memorable simile, the Buddha explains to
Venerable Ānanda how the non-returner cuts through the
five lower fetters.

16   'There is a path, Ānanda, a way for the abandoning of the five lower fetters. That someone, without
coming to that path, that way, could know or see or
abandon the five lower fetters [thereby becoming a
non-returner]: that is not possible. Just as when there

---

4   AN 9.44
5   MN 70.16, SN 12.70; cp. AN 4.87

is a great tree with heartwood standing, it is not possible that anyone could cut out the heartwood without first cutting through the bark and sapwood... But that someone, by coming to that path, that way, could know and see and abandon the five lower fetters: that is possible.

17   'And what, Ānanda, is that path? Here, with seclusion from belongings, the abandoning of unbeneficial qualities, the complete tranquilization of bodily disturbance, quite secluded from sensual pleasures, secluded from unbeneficial qualities, a monk enters and abides in the first jhāna... second jhāna... third jhāna... fourth jhāna... base of infinite space... base of infinite consciousness... base of nothingness. Whatever exists in there of feeling, perception, conceptual activities, and consciousness [also physical form in the four jhānas only], he sees those phenomena as impermanent, suffering, a disease, a tumor, a barb, a calamity, an affliction, alien, disintegrating, empty, not-self. He turns his mind away from those phenomena and directs it towards the deathless element thus: "This is peaceful, this is sublime; that is, the samatha of all activities, the relinquishment of all belongings, the evaporation of craving, fading away, cessation, Nibbana." Standing on that he attains the evaporation of the poisons [or to the state of non-return]... This is the path, the way for the abandoning of the five lower fetters.'

18   'In that case, Bhante, how is it that some monks are released of heart and some are released by understanding?'

19   'The difference here, Ānanda, is in their spiritual faculties, I say.'[6]

---

[6]   MN 64.7ff.

20   Here again the simile drives home that not only is each
stage of the path absolutely necessary, it is just as necessary that they occur in the correct sequence: first the bark,
then the sapwood, then the heartwood. The samādhi here
occurs with the 'tranquilizing of bodily disturbance', which
as usual is obviously not referring to a 'path-moment' of
samādhi.[7] This is confirmed yet again in the body of the text,
which treats samādhi exclusively as a basis for vipassanā,
not as an enlightenment experience.

21   The suttas do not record any similarly forceful, definitive statements about the samādhi required by the other
'trainees' (*sekha*)—the stream-enterer, the once-returner,
and those on the way—yet the basic position is straightforward.

22   'Here, a monk is endowed with the right view, right
intention, right speech, right action, right livelihood,
right effort, right mindfulness, and right samādhi of a
trainee. That is what "trainee" refers to.'[8]

23   'For a long time, Bhante, I have understood the Dhamma taught by the Blessed One thus: there is knowledge
for one with samādhi, not for one without samādhi.
But which comes first, samādhi or knowledge?'

24   ...'Mahānāma, the virtue, samādhi, and understanding of both the trainee and the adept have been spoken
of by the Blessed One... And what is the samādhi of the
trainee? Here, a monk... enters and abides in the first
jhāna... second jhāna... third jhāna... fourth jhāna.'[9]

25   Without hesitation or prevarication, Venerable Ānanda
states that the samādhi of the trainee—that is, all *ariyas* or

---

[7]   *Duṭṭhulla*, sometimes rendered 'inertia', but one cannot tranquilize
inertia.

[8]   SN 45.13

[9]   AN 3.73

'noble ones' except the arahant—is the four jhānas. Ānanda's answer to Mahānāma's question is not so explicit, but it seems to imply that the samādhi of the trainee comes before the understanding of the trainee, but the understanding of the trainee comes before the samādhi of the adept.

26   Such forthright and direct statements that the trainee possesses jhāna are by no means rare. Here are some more examples.

27   'One trains in the higher virtue, the higher mind, and the higher understanding, therefore a monk is called a trainee.'[10]

28   'What is the training in the higher mind? Here, a monk... enters and abides in the first jhāna... second jhāna... third jhāna... fourth jhāna.'[11]

29   'And what is a true person? Here, someone is of right view, right intention, right speech, right action, right livelihood, right effort, right mindfulness, and right samādhi.'[12]

30   'How is a person an unshakable contemplative [i.e. a stream-enterer]? Here a monk has right view, right intention, right speech, right action, right livelihood, right effort, right mindfulness, and right samādhi.'[13]

31   'Sāriputta, one who is endowed with this noble eight-fold path is called a stream-enterer, this venerable one of such and such a name and clan.'[14]

32   'Here, a monk has fulfilled virtue and has measure of samādhi and understanding... with the evaporation of three fetters he is a stream-enterer...'[15]

---

[10]   AN 3.84; cp. MN 48.12
[11]   AN 3.88, 89
[12]   SN 45.25
[13]   AN 4.89
[14]   SN 55.5
[15]   AN 3.86, 9.12

33   'A faithful noble disciple, having thus repeatedly
      practiced striving, remembering, samādhi, and un-
      derstanding, has full confidence thus: "These princi-
      ples which I had previously only heard about I now
      abide in having personally contacted, and see having
      penetrated with understanding."'[16]

34   There is little room for equivocation in all these passages.
      A stream- enterer possesses the path, including jhāna as
      right samādhi.

35   Sometimes the Buddha described the wrong eightfold
      path as the 'bad path'.[17] Since samādhi is the culmination of
      the path, the bad path is the absence of samādhi.

36   'Samādhi is the path; no samādhi is the bad path.'[18]

37   And, as one would expect, it is impossible to attain the no-
      ble stages while still cultivating the 'bad path'. More specifi-
      cally, however, the following passage speaks of identity view,
      doubt, and misapprehension of virtue & vows, which are
      the three fetters that are abandoned by the stream-enterer.

38   'Without abandoning paying attention away from
      the root, cultivating the bad path, and laziness of the
      heart, it is impossible to abandon identity view, doubt,
      and misapprehension of virtue & vows.'[19]

39   If the 'path' by which these three fetters are abandoned by
      the streamenterer is, or more modestly, includes samādhi,
      then those on the path to stream-entry must also possess
      samādhi.

---

[16]   SN 48.50
[17]   MN 19.26
[18]   AN 6.64
[19]   AN 10.76

40 Being destined for enlightenment,[20] these individuals are of great interest to the aspirant, although since the Theravāda tradition relegates them to the status of a 'mind moment' they are often overlooked. If they possess jhāna it follows as a matter of course that those at higher stages will too. Let us see what the suttas have to say about these individuals. They are regularly credited with the five spiritual faculties.

41   'One who has completely fulfilled these five spiritual faculties is an arahant. If they are weaker, he is one on the way to witnessing the fruit of arahantship. If they are weaker than that he is a non-returner... one on the way to non-returning... a once-returner... one on the way to once-returning... a stream-enterer... If they are weaker than that, he is one on the way to witnessing the fruit of stream-entry. But monks, I say that one in whom these five spiritual faculties are completely and totally absent is an outsider, one who stands in the faction of ordinary persons.'[21]

42 So the one on the way to stream-entry possesses the spiritual faculty of samādhi, in other words jhāna, albeit weakly. 'Weakly' is of course quite different from 'not at all'. An accomplished practitioner is one who can enter such states at will, whenever they want, for as long as they want, and in whatever manner they want. Those on the path to stream-entry need not possess such a mastery, but they must have some experience of the path. Below we will examine several passages that describe those on the way to stream-entry in detail, which help to clarify what is meant by 'weakly'.

43 The one on the path to stream-entry is further described as the 'Dhamma-follower' and the 'faith-follower'. These

---

[20] MN 22.46
[21] SN 48.18

terms are most commonly used to distinguish between those
on the way to stream-entry as giving chief emphasis to either understanding or faith. However, in a few passages
they seem to be undifferentiated, such that the two terms
apply to all those on the path to stream-entry treated as
a single group.[22] In fact, the suttas' treatment of the different classifications of noble individuals (apart from the
standard set of four pairs) is somewhat loose, and must be
sensitively judged in each context. Even when they are dif-
ferentiated, the Dhamma-follower has the spiritual faculty
of faith, while the faith-follower has the spiritual faculty of
understanding, leaving no doubt that the difference is simply a matter of emphasis, and explaining how both terms
can also be applied to all those on the path to stream-entry
without distinction.

44   The following passage compares the Dhamma-follower
and the faith-follower with the stream-enterer. In this passage, the term 'rightness' refers to the noble eightfold path.[23]

45   'Monks, the eye... the ear... the nose... the tongue...
        the body... the mind is impermanent, changing, be-
        coming otherwise. One who has faith and certainty
        in these principles thus is called a faith-follower, one
        who has entered the fixed course of rightness, entered
        the plane of true persons, and transcended the plane
        of ordinary persons. He is incapable of doing any ac-
        tion having done which he would be reborn in hell, an
        animal's womb, or the ghost realm. He is incapable of
        passing away without having witnessed the fruit of
        stream-entry.

---

[22] E.g. MN 22.46, MN 34.10. This is reminiscent of the usage of the anal-
ogous terms 'release of heart, release by understanding' which we
briefly noted above (Chapter 2.11).

[23] SN 45.21

46   'Monks, the eye... the ear... the nose... the tongue...
       the body... the mind is impermanent, changing, becom-
       ing otherwise. One who thus accepts these principles
       after pondering with a measure of understanding is
       called a Dhamma-follower, one who has entered the
       fixed course of rightness, entered the plane of true
       persons, and transcended the plane of ordinary per-
       sons. He is incapable of doing any action having done
       which he would be reborn in hell, an animal's womb,
       or the ghost realm. He is incapable of passing away
       without having witnessed the fruit of stream-entry.

47   'One who knows & sees these principles thus is called
       a stream-enterer, not subject to [rebirth in] the abyss,
       fixed in destiny, destined for enlightenment.'[24]

48   While the above passage deals with the understanding of
       those on the path to stream-entry, the following deals with
       their samādhi.

49   'What kind of person is the Dhamma-follower? Here,
       monks, a certain person does not, having transcended
       forms, personally contact and abide in those peaceful
       formless liberations, and his poisons are not fully evap-
       orated after being seen with understanding. But he
       accepts after pondering with a measure of understand-
       ing the principles made known by the Tathāgata, and
       he has these qualities: the spiritual faculties of faith,
       energy, mindfulness, samādhi, and understanding...

50   'What kind of person is the faith-follower? Here,
       monks, a certain person does not, having transcended
       forms, personally contact and abide in those peaceful
       formless liberations, and his poisons are not fully evap-
       orated after being seen with understanding. But he
       has a measure of faith and affection for the Tathāgata,
       and he has these qualities: the spiritual faculties of

---

[24] SN 25.1

faith, energy, mindfulness, samādhi, and understanding ...'[25]

51   Once more, these individuals on the path to stream entry
are said to possess the spiritual faculty of samādhi, the four
jhānas.

52   In the following passage, 'laughing understanding' and
'swift understanding' refer to the arahant and the non re-
turner, 'release' to the arahant only. Although the terms are
not used, the first 'certain person' is obviously the Dhamma-follower, and the second is the faith-follower.

53   'Here, Mahānāma, a certain person is endowed neither with confirmed confidence in the Buddha, Dhamma, and Sangha, nor with laughing understanding,
swift understanding, or release. Yet he has these qualities: the spiritual faculties of faith, energy, mindfulness, samādhi, and understanding; and he accepts the
Dhamma made known by the Tathāgata after pondering with a measure of understanding. Even this person
will not go to hell, an animal's womb, the ghost realm,
or to a lower realm, bad destiny, or the abyss.

54   'Here, Mahānāma, a certain person is endowed neither with confirmed confidence in the Buddha, Dhamma, and Sangha, nor with laughing understanding,
swift understanding, or release. Yet he has these qualities: the spiritual faculties of faith, energy, mindfulness, samādhi, and understanding; and he has a measure of faith and affection for the Tathāgata. Even this
person will not go to hell, an animal's womb, the ghost
realm, or to a lower realm, bad destiny, or the abyss.'[26]

55   Those on the way to stream-entry are not contrasted with
the streamenterer in terms of their level of samādhi. Both

---

[25] MN 70.20–21
[26] SN 55.24

classes of people will possess the spiritual faculty of samādhi, or jhāna. The difference is in how they understand
Dhamma. The stream-enterer 'knows & sees' directly, while
those on the path to stream-entry accept by faith or by pondering, i.e. with primarily emotive or intellectual acquiescence to the teachings.

56   These kinds of acceptance are two of five ways of knowing mentioned elsewhere, which may lead to either right or
wrong conclusions, and which do not constitute 'awakening
to the truth'. However, if correctly apprehended—as provisional, not conclusive—they form part of the practice for
awakening.[27] In fact, acquiescence in line with the teachings
is necessary before one can enter the way.[28]

57   Although this contrast is consistent with the normal as-
cription of 'knowledge & vision in accordance with reality'
to the stream-enterer, elsewhere the noble ones as a whole
are described as 'directly knowing' in contrast with the ordinary person, who merely 'perceives'.[29]

58   Rather than describing those on the path to stream-entry
as directly knowing or not, perhaps they are better described
as being in the process of coming to know. Like the time just
before sunrise: compared with midnight it is light, but compared with midday it is still dark. When contrasted with the
ordinary person, then, it may be said that they have direct
knowledge, but when contrasted with the stream-enterer
their knowledge is primarily conceptual. The possession
of the spiritual faculty of understanding, though limited
in this way, implies a degree of direct introspective insight.
Not having fully seen the Dhamma, they also lack 'confirmed

---

[27] MN 95.14*ff*.; cp. SN 12.68.
[28] AN 6.88, AN 6.98*ff*.
[29] E.g. MN 1, SN 48.5.

confidence'. Earlier, we saw this as a key ingredient of the 'relinquishment' that supports the samādhi of the stream-enterer. Those on the path to stream -entry would instead rely on their own intrinsic qualities: love of the Buddha, freedom from doubt about the teachings, and lack of remorse for doing evil.

59   While the texts exhibit some equivocation over the understanding and faith faculties of those on the way to stream-entry, no such hesitation is expressed regarding their samādhi faculty. The Buddha specifically addresses the question of the level of samādhi required for the initial entry to the path. In common with the arahant released by understanding (sometimes), those on the path to stream-entry do not have the formless liberations. But they are repeatedly declared to possess the spiritual faculty of samādhi, i.e. jhāna. Although the Buddha took pains to make the attainment of the way to stream-entry appear accessible, emphasizing the qualities that the Dhamma-follower and faith-follower lack, nowhere is jhāna included among the qualities that they lack.

60   The weakness of the spiritual faculty of samādhi may be explained by the weakness of the supporting 'relinquishment'. The weakness of the faculty, it may be noted, does not necessarily imply weakness of samādhi. Even ordinary people, while totally bereft of the faculties, may be highly skilled in all samādhi attainments. The term 'spiritual faculty' implies rather that these principles become the ascendant prevailing dispositions, dominant in their own fields, and not to be overthrown. For ordinarily people, the long-term prognosis is decline from the heights they have attained, and eventually perhaps rebirth even in hell; while for the trainees,

though they may still have short-term difficulties, the long term will bring only progress.

61   If those on the path to stream-entry possess jhāna, why then, as we saw above, is samādhi not directly stated in the dependent liberation to be a vital condition for this attainment? This is an abstruse question, and in the absence of a direct statement from the suttas, we might be forgiven for thinking that it is little more than a slight vagueness in wording. And yet, as so often in the Dhamma, there is a delicate logic at play here.

62   Consider the structure of the noble eightfold path. One starts with conceptual right view, and then develops the remaining factors culminating in right samādhi, which includes reviewing knowledge, a wisdom practice. At this point all the path factors have been fulfilled to a degree which may for some be sufficient for entering the way. So it seems that the attainment of right samādhi may itself be equivalent to entering the way. So it could not be a condition for entering the way, since nothing can be a condition for itself. This does not necessarily imply that all those with right view who develop samādhi become noble ones; this would depend on one's spiritual maturity, especially one's depth of wisdom or faith.

63   Since those on the path to stream-entry must attain stream-entry in this very life, even if prevented from practicing by, say, grave illness or sudden death, it is difficult to escape the conclusion that they need not further develop their meditation after the entry to the path. This is because the attainment of the path requires development of all the path factors to a sufficient degree, such that the conditions for stream-entry are already fulfilled, requiring only time to bear their fruit. There does not seem to be any method given to ascer-

tain exactly how much the path factors must be developed to reach this point. Normally, of course, the character of such individuals would be to delight in meditation, and the Buddha further exhorts them to put forth effort to minimize their time in saṁsāra.

Conclusion

64 All noble ones are consistently and repeatedly said to be endowed with samādhi as a path-factor and spiritual faculty, to possess the samādhi of a trainee, and to train in the higher mind. These are all defined as jhāna.

65 The conclusion is inescapable: jhāna is necessary for all the stages of noble liberation. The noble path has eight factors. Jhānas are one of those factors. Only with the fulfillment of all eight factors can one be considered to be on the path.

66 At the end of our tour of the suttas we return to this simple, straightforward principle. Our explorations of the subtle, sometimes enigmatic, world of the suttas serve to illuminate this model, revealing unexpected nuances, unappreciated depths. But always and everywhere, the keynote of peace permeates the path.

67 'I say, monk, that the evaporation of the poisons is dependent on the first jhāna... second jhāna... third jhāna... fourth jhāna... base of infinite space... base of infinite consciousness... base of nothingness... base of neither perception nor non-perception... cessation of perception and feeling.'[30]

---

[30] AN 9.36

Chapter 8

Counterexamples

HAVING COMPLETED OUR SURVEY, we now turn to a discussion of some of the sutta passages that have been taken to indicate that jhānas are not necessary for liberation. We have seen that the suttas explain the path clearly and explicitly, approaching the subject from different angles, but always including jhāna as an intrinsic element. If we are to discover a jhāna-less path we should expect a similar approach.

2   The principle of proportion and the principle of historical perspective, which I proposed in the first chapter, now come to the fore. Minor teachings should be seen in context. Background stories should be carefully examined for authenticity. We should ask: 'Is the Buddha altering the eightfold path, or describing a different path? Or is he clarifying details, emphasizing particular aspects or modes of practicing the eightfold path?'

3   As far as I can see, there are two possible outcomes of this discussion. Either the counter-examples do not imply that

jhānas are unnecessary, or there is a contradiction in the teachings. We must remain alive to both possible outcomes. In most cases difficulties are readily solvable. If, however, the interpretations we provide—some of which must be tentative in the absence of definitive statements in the passages themselves, itself an indication of their secondary status— are not felt to be acceptable in some cases, we cannot simply ignore the authoritative sutta passages in the previous chapters.

4   The Susīma Sutta has been frequently relied on to substantiate the claim that an arahant need not possess jhāna. According to the Pali version of the sutta, the wanderer Susīma fraudulently entered the Sangha desiring wealth and fame. He questioned a number of monks who had declared arahantship, and they denied possessing psychic powers or formless attainments. This is quite in line with the general position of the suttas. Jhāna is not mentioned, although as always it is implied if the sutta is read in the light of other sutta statements. For example, their declaration of arahantship included the phrase, 'The holy life has been lived,' which means they have fully developed the noble eightfold path. They say they are 'released by understanding'; we have seen above that such an attainment regularly includes jhāna, although, as here, it may not include the formless attainments, which are extra and beyond the four jhānas.

5   Venerable Susīma is obviously puzzled by the monks' statements, since he appears to think the goal of Buddhist practice was the realization of psychic powers or formless attainments, which was, it seems, a common belief among non-Buddhists at the time. He goes to the Buddha. The Bud-

dha does not explicitly endorse the monks' claims to arahantship,[1] but explains the situation thus:

6   'First there is the knowledge of the regularity of
     natural principles; afterwards there is the knowledge
     of Nibbana.'[2]

7   This statement re-emphasizes the importance of causality and the regular sequence of knowledge. Without an understanding of the causal principles underlying suffering
and the causal principles of the practice to break free from
suffering, it is impossible to realize Nibbana. The Buddha
then teaches Venerable Susīma a passage from the Anattalakkhaṇa Sutta culminating in the release of arahantship.[3]
This release is described in the Anattalakkhaṇa Sutta as 'release of mind'. We saw above that this 'mind' (or 'heart')
release is due to the fading away of lust; and the fading
away of lust is due to the development of the mind through
samatha.[4] The Buddha goes on to teach dependent origination. Susīma says that he understands those teachings, and
filled with remorse, confesses his transgression to the Buddha.

8   Interestingly, in the Chinese version of this text, though
the basic doctrinal teaching of dependent origination is similar and so original, the background story is quite different.
There, Venerable Susīma, having fraudulently entered the
Sangha, nevertheless quickly picked up enough doctrinal
knowledge to expose by cross-examining some monks who
had falsely boasted of being enlightened (one of the most
serious vinaya offenses). As this text shows the monks in a

[1]   See MN 105.
[2]   SN 12.70
[3]   SN 22.59
[4]   AN 2.3.10, quoted above.

very bad light it is unlikely to have been forged. While the
faults of monks are of necessity on display throughout the
Vinaya Piṭaka, the suttas almost always focus on the positive. Perhaps the background story in the Pali version was
rewritten to whitewash faults in the Sangha. This must have
occurred when the Pali canon of the Theravāda school had already become separated from the version later preserved in
Chinese. This separation occurred no earlier than the Third
Council, over a century after the Buddha's passing away.[5]
This reinforces the principle that we should not use such
isolated cases to overthrow the central teachings, which
are all found in nearly identical form in all early Buddhist
traditions.

In several places the Buddha talks about two 'ways of practice', which may be taken to indicate the distinction between
separate meditative paths on the basis of whether or not
they include jhāna. The 'painful way of practice' consists of
the perceptions of the ugliness of the body, the repulsive-
ness of food, boredom with the whole world, death, and the
impermanence of all activities. This 'painful way of practice'
is contrasted (unfavorably) with the 'pleasant way of practice', which consists of jhāna.[6] We may note that the painful
mode is never identified with vipassanā; the basic purpose
of most of these contemplations is to eradicate sensual lust,
which is an aspect of samatha. Nor has it anything to do with
contemplation of painful feelings. Moreover, the distinction
between these ways of practice was clearly not meant as a

---

[5]   This information is from Richard Gombrich's *How Buddhism Began*,
   which includes a chapter attempting to trace the beginnings of the
   decline of samādhi to the period after the Buddha's passing away, when
   the teachings were being collated and organized. He uses a different
   logic to arrive at a similar date as I give in the text.

[6]   AN 4.163

hard and fast division. Venerable Sāriputta's practice was of the pleasant mode, yet he had also perfected body contemplation.[7] Venerable Moggallāna's practice was of the painful mode, yet he possessed mastery in all levels of samādhi.[8] The distinction is merely a matter of emphasis. The pleasant practice of jhāna does not supplant the other seven path factors; nor does the painful practice supplant jhāna. In fact, one practicing each of the contemplations of the painful way of practice is said to 'not neglect jhāna'[9] and to possess the five spiritual faculties, if only weakly.[10]

10 Another passage that has been evoked to demonstrate the superfluity of jhāna is when the Buddha says to Mahānāma the Sakyan that sensuality may arise in a noble one if they do not attain jhāna.[11] However, this is phrased in the present tense, 'does not attain', not 'has never attained'. It seems that even after a stream-enterer has seen the Dhamma their samādhi may fall away unless they devote sufficient time to meditation, and therefore certain defilements may rearise.[12] Stream-enterers and once-returners are not 'perfected in samādhi'. This does not imply that they have never experienced any jhānas, only that they may not have experienced all four jhānas, or may not be proficient in them.

11 Again, the six recollections—the Buddha, Dhamma, Sangha, virtue, generosity, and deities—are taught as a basis for arahantship,[13] even though according to the Visuddhimagga they only lead to access samādhi. Some teachers have ar-

---

[7] AN 4.168, AN 9.11
[8] AN 4.167, SN 40.1–9
[9] AN 1.20
[10] AN 4.162
[11] MN 14.4, quoted above.
[12] Cp. SN 55.40, quoted above.
[13] AN 6.26

gued that this shows that arahantship need not be based on jhāna. It seems to me more than a little desperate to invoke such suttas, which teach samatha for arahantship with no mention of vipassanā, in order to establish a path of 'pure vipassanā'.

12   Moreover, the Visuddhimagga's claim that these practices do not lead to jhāna is not sustainable. The suttas say that these meditations will abandon the five cords of sensual pleasures, so that the meditator dwells 'with heart become in every way like space—vast, exalted, measureless, free from hatred and ill will.'[14] They are called 'blissful abidings here & now pertaining to the higher mind, for the purification of the unpurified mind, for the brightening of the dull mind.'[15] They lead to the abandoning of the 'taints of the mind'.[16] Each of these phrases implies jhāna. We cannot distinguish based on the suttas between the samādhi which results from these recollections and the samādhi which results from any other meditation subject. The Buddha simply confirms this straight-forward interpretation by saying that one who develops these recollections 'does not neglect jhāna'.[17]

13   The chief reason why the Visuddhimagga thinks these recollections cannot induce jhāna is that they involve recollecting and pondering over diverse qualities of the Buddha, etc., and so can lead only to access samādhi (which is an incidental admission that so-called access samādhi is not truly one-pointed).[18] But there seems to be no reason why one could not leave off contemplating diverse qualities and

---

[14]   AN 6.26
[15]   AN 5.179
[16]   AN 3.70
[17]   AN 1.20
[18]   Vsm 7.67

focus on just one quality to arouse jhāna. A similar process is recommended in the Visuddhimagga itself for some other meditations, such as the parts of the body. This technique, based on the mental recitation of the word 'buddho', is a favorite method for developing jhāna in contemporary Thailand.

14 Probably the most striking and influential passages, which many believe to imply the superfluity of jhāna, are the background stories of monastics and laypeople attaining various levels of Dhamma with no mention of prior meditative development, usually while listening to a talk. There is usually nothing to positively rule out the possibility of previous attainment of jhāna, but in many cases this seems unlikely. Regarded as extraordinary and noteworthy, such cases of 'instant enlightenment' occur in a small proportion of suttas (for example, about half a dozen times in the Majjhima Nikāya), almost always when the Buddha himself is teaching. The Buddha is, however, rarely personally credited with confirming these attainments. In fact, he is at times reluctant to do so, typically preferring to show how one can know for oneself.[19]

15 The most common attainment is stream-entry, so many conclude that such passages imply that this does not require jhāna. There are, however, a number of striking descriptions of people attaining arahantship in circumstances where it seems unlikely they had previously developed jhāna. So it seems that if such stories imply a jhāna-less stream-enterer we must also admit a jhāna-less arahant. But I prefer to reverse the logic: the texts unequivocally declare that arahants must have jhāna, so these stories cannot prove the existence

---

[19] DN 16.2.8

of jhāna-less arahants. This being so, they cannot prove the jhāna-less stream-enterer either.

16   I will advance three lines of argument to support this conclusion. Firstly, such stories are often of questionable authenticity. Secondly, they frequently describe a kind of samādhi gained immediately prior to the enlightenment experience that could well be jhāna. And thirdly, they were meant to point to the path, not replace it.

17   First to historical matters. Descriptions of 'instant enlightenment' are scattered through the canon. Typically they are part of a narrative background. Such narratives, unlike the doctrinal teachings, are not ascribed to the Buddha or his disciples. They appear in the texts, author or authors unknown, time or times of composition unknown, source or sources unknown. Who was it that knew what stage of enlightenment had been reached by these people at that time? It is understandable that devoted students of a great teacher like the Buddha would listen well and remember, with a reasonable degree of agreement, the words that are spoken on an occasion. But a degree of refined spiritual attainment is not so easy to discern.

18   It should come as no surprise, then, that in comparing suttas in Pali and Chinese, we find that, again and again, the content of the teaching is essentially the same, while the degree of attainment of the listeners should be completely different. After hearing the same talk, in one version the hearer is said to become a stream-enterer, while in another he goes forth and becomes an arahant; or else in one version he merely listens with appreciation, while in another he takes the three refuges.

19   This reminds us of the basic fact, so obvious that it is almost always overlooked: such declarations of attainment

are not 'the suttas spoken by the Buddha'. They are framing narratives which are meant to give a context to the suttas spoken by the Buddha.

20   These stories appear most characteristically in the first chapter of the Vinaya Mahāvagga. I will therefore concentrate on this text, though many of the features I note here also occur in other contexts.

21   This chapter tells of the founding of Buddhism. It starts under the Bodhi tree with the Buddha reflecting how Dhammas become clear to the 'ardent brahman in jhāna'. It goes on to tell how the Buddha converted his first followers and established a monastic order, thus serving to introduce the Vinaya. Together with the Mahā Parinibbāna Sutta—with which it shares much in common—this text forms the basis of all later biographies of the Buddha. The other early schools also had their versions of this text, some of them extending it to a full-fledged biography. Although the early suttas spare little time for biography, later writers found that the Buddha's life story gave the teachings that 'personal touch' ideal for popularizing the teachings. The story was probably included to provide the Vinaya students with some background and doctrinal teachings, rounding out their education.

22   And, adding zest to the sometimes dry Vinaya material, the chapter abounds in all manner of wonderful and marvelous happenings—deities appearing; displays of supernormal powers; the Buddha even does battle with a ferocious fire-breathing dragon, tames it, and puts it in his bowl! This latter event comes replete with a flowery but superfluous verse summary[20]—an obviously late literary feature. Accounts of miraculous events are fairly restrained in the

---

[20] Mistaken for prose in the PTS Pali and translation.

early strata of the canon. They increase markedly in the later strata, and proliferate wildly in later literature.

23   Not least wonderful and marvelous are the 'miracles of conversion'. It is to be expected that the codifiers of a religion should ascribe the maximum possible purity to the first adherents. It seems that almost everyone the Buddha taught in those first months became a stream-enterer at least. This includes, for example, King Bimbisāra together with a hundred thousand leading householders of Magadha. (There is no mention of how such a vast multitude managed to squeeze around the woodland shrine where the Buddha was staying.) Such trends, too, proliferated in later writings; the Milinda Pañha piously informs us that over a billion lay followers had realized the Dhamma. There is surely an anomaly here. Only a short while before, the Buddha, reflecting on the subtlety of Dhamma and the strength of defilements, doubted anyone could understand and famously hesitated whether to teach at all.

24   A. K. Warder suspects a political influence at work here. Although the Buddha's main center of operations was in the neighboring kingdom of Kosala, there are no comparable accounts of mass realizations there. During the period this text was being assembled, the star of Kosala was waning, while that of Magadha was waxing, following the aggressive expansionist policy initiated by Ajātasattu and culminating in the pan-Indian Buddhist empire of Asoka. It would have been most agreeable for the increasingly politicized Sangha of the time to emphasize the early Buddhist traditions of Magadha. In this chapter's emphasis on biography, missionary activity, miracles, mass lay conversion, and the liberating effect of listening to teachings there is a close connection

with the popular, urbanized, scholastic Buddhism which emerged in Asoka's time.

25   I suggest that this first chapter of the Mahāvagga was finalized in the same period as the final chapter of the Cūḷavagga, which tells of the Second Council, one hundred years after the Buddha's passing away. Although the doctrinal seeds around which this text crystallized—the four noble truths, the eightfold noble path, dependent origination—spring from the heart of the Buddha's awakening, the details of the connecting biography record popular tradition as much as enlightened revelation. And while the popular narrative appears to depict people gaining stream-entry with no prior meditative practice, the doctrinal teachings that inspire those realizations are just the same as everywhere else: the eightfold path, four noble truths, dependent origination.

26   As I have already noted, 'instant enlightenment' also occurs elsewhere in the Pali canon. Having seen the dubious authenticity of the text where these events occur most prominently, we may well suspect that other occurrences may be tarred with the same brush. Stories come to mind such as the conversion of the assassins sent by Devadatta and the later conversion of Devadatta's entire retinue.

27   Now, I do not wish to suggest that all such stories are spurious. Some of the doctrinal passages we will examine below suggest that it is possible to realize Dhamma during a talk, and who knows whether any of the historical accounts may be genuine. However, I do wish to suggest that the historical evidence attesting to realization without prior practice is slim. It is often just those occasions when it seems least likely that the listener would have previously developed jhāna that turn out to be most historically questionable.

28   And so to my second line of argument. The passages describing 'instant enlightenment' frequently emphasize how
the joy of listening to Dhamma purifies the mind in readi-
ness for realization. Although the texts are not completely
explicit on this point, the description of this mind state is
certainly consonant with jhāna. The standard passage is as
follows.

29   'Then the Blessed One gave the householder Upāli
graduated instruction; that is, talk on giving, virtue,
and the heavens. He explained the danger, degrada-
tion, and defilement in sensual pleasures and the bless-
ings of renunciation. When he knew that the householder Upāli's mind was ready, soft, free of hindrances,
elated, clear of doubt, he expounded to him the special teaching of the Buddhas: Suffering, its origin, its
cessation, and the path. Just as a clean cloth with all
the stains removed would take dye evenly, so too while
Upāli was sitting right there, the stainless, immaculate
eye of the Dhamma arose in him: "Whatever is subject
to arising is subject to cessation."'[21]

30   This passage emphasizes the gradual, progressive nature
of the teaching, paralleling the gradual, progressive nature
of the path. We have seen how jhānas, the 'bliss of renunciation', are the escape from sensual pleasures; how the freedom from hindrances is equated with the first jhāna; and
how samādhi is the indispensable condition for seeing the
four noble truths. We have also seen that a stream-enterer
knows that: 'These principles, which I formerly only heard
of, I now abide in having personally contacted, and see having penetrated with understanding.' The simile of the clean
cloth further emphasizes the need for purity of mind to see

---

[21] MN 56.18

the Dhamma. Is it possible to attain jhāna during a Dhamma talk?

31   'When a noble disciple bends his ear to listen to Dhamma, paying full attention as a matter of vital concern, applying his whole heart to it, on that occasion the five hindrances are not present, on that occasion the seven enlightenment factors come to fulfillment by development.'[22]

32   Here, samādhi is signified in both the negative aspect, as abandonment of the hindrances, and positive aspect, as fulfillment—not mere preliminary arousing—of the enlightenment factor of samādhi. I do not see how this could be anything less than full jhāna. While the above passage concerns one who is already a noble disciple, the following passage concerns one who is to enter the way to stream-entry.[23]

33   'Endowed with these five qualities, monks, one listening to the true Dhamma is incapable of entering the fixed course of rightness regarding beneficial qualities. What five? One criticizes the teachings; one criticizes the teacher; one criticizes oneself; one listens to Dhamma as one of scattered mind, not of one-pointed mind; and one pays attention away from the root. [But if one has the opposite qualities, one is capable.]'[24]

34   If one-pointedness here merely implies paying full attention to the teaching, this passage might be read as implying that a pre-jhanic level of concentration can be sufficient to realize the Dhamma while listening to a discourse. But 'rightness' means the noble eightfold path, including jhāna; and the samādhi of one practicing for stream-entry is the spiritual faculty of samādhi, etc. We have also noted that the

---

[22] SN 46.38
[23] Cp. SN 25, quoted above.
[24] AN 5.151

only passage that analyzes an unambiguously pre-jhanic samādhi in more detail describes it as 'not unified'.[25] This passage therefore seems to imply jhāna attained either before or during the talk itself. If so, this strongly supports the necessity of jhāna for entering the path. The following passage describes the process in more detail.

35   'There are these five bases for release where for a monk abiding diligent, ardent, and resolute his unreleased mind becomes released, his unevaporated poisons become evaporated, and the unattained supreme security from bondage becomes attained. What five?

36   'Here, the Teacher or a respected companion in the holy life teaches the Dhamma to a monk...

37   '... Or a monk teaches the Dhamma he has learnt to others...

38   '... Or a monk recites in detail the Dhamma he has learnt...

39   '... Or a monk thinks over, examines, and explores with his mind the Dhamma he has learnt...

40   '... Or a certain basis of samādhi is well apprehended, well attended to, well held in mind, and well penetrated with understanding...

41   [In all of the above cases:] 'He is inspired by the meaning and the Dhamma. Being inspired by the meaning and the Dhamma, gladness is born in him. In one who is glad, rapture is born. In one with rapturous mind, the body becomes tranquil. One with tranquil body feels bliss. The mind of one who is blissful enters samādhi... These are the five bases of release...'[26]

42   These situations correspond with the development of the enlightenment factors,[27] with the basis of psychic power

---

[25] AN 3.110, quoted above.
[26] AN 5.26
[27] SN 46.3

'dependent on inquiry, one gains samādhi, one gains one-pointedness of mind', with the path which develops vipassanā prior to samatha, and with the nine dhammas that are very helpful.[28] The crucial conditions for jhāna are present exactly as normal, and samādhi, the regular synonym for jhāna, appears as usual in between bliss and liberating insight.

43   Unlike the previous passages, here there is no particular reason to suppose that the attainment of samādhi must be simultaneous with hearing the Dhamma, etc. Rather, hearing the Dhamma, etc., is the spark for the development of samādhi. Although we noted above that the historical records almost always associate such events with teachings given by the Buddha himself, these doctrinal passages do not distinguish between whether the Buddha or a disciple is teaching; nor do they imply that the teacher must have psychic powers. We may note that only once in the suttas does a monk become enlightened while teaching, and in that case the monk was already a non-returner.[29] In fact, listening to Dhamma is the only one of these occasions mentioned regularly for attaining stream-entry; but we should be cautious in drawing any implications from this. The suttas are, after all, records of oral teachings, not of meditation experiences.

44   This passage should be considered together with the discourse on the 'abider in Dhamma'.[30] There, the first four kinds of monks—the studier, the teacher, the reciter, and the thinker—are contrasted unfavorably with the 'abider in Dhamma', who 'does not neglect retreat, is devoted to

---

[28] DN 34.2.2
[29] SN 22.89
[30] AN 5.73

samatha of the heart within'. Study only yields its fruits when married to meditation.

45   The case of the brahman Dhānañjāni might also be mentioned in this connection. A corrupt tax collector, he was nevertheless able to develop the divine abidings on his deathbed through being exhorted by Venerable Sāriputta, and through the attainment of that jhāna he was reborn in the Brahmā realm.[31]

46   Taking all these passages together, it seems that it may be possible for certain people to attain jhāna during a Dhamma teaching, and to use this for developing insight leading to liberation.

47   I have left the most important line of argument until last. These passages were never intended to supplant or modify the noble eightfold path. Their purpose is to inspire, to rouse, to point to the teachings. They should encourage us to investigate the teachings thoroughly and to apply our whole hearts to the practice for the realization of the Dhamma in its fullness. Let us not grab the snake by its tail. Exploiting such passages to opt out of key aspects of the path surely confounds the very purpose of the teachings.

48   When all is said and done, though, these passages remain the most difficult to square with the integral importance of jhāna in the path. Indeed, they rest uneasily with our basic understanding that the attainment of Dhamma is a direct inner realization transcending concepts. At some point in the discourse, surely, the listener must apply the conceptual knowledge they have gained to the direct contemplation of experience. This much is implied by 'paying attention to the root'. If this inner turning to vipassanā can occur, there seems to be no hard and fast reason why an inner turning

---

[31]   MN 97

to jhāna cannot also occur.[32] Certainly, there are no sutta passages that rule this out. Perhaps we must simply accept that these are almost unimaginable events occurring for the most extraordinary individuals.

49   For practical purposes, the question as to whether or not such events imply jhāna is perhaps not of overriding importance. At most they establish that some individuals can make extremely rapid progress on the path. They never constitute a separate path. The best way to maximize our chance of realizing Dhamma while listening to a talk is to assiduously develop samatha and vipassanā. Right view is assisted not just by learning, and not just by meditation, but by 'virtue, learning (or 'listening'), discussion, samatha, and vipassanā'.[33]

50   The above passages all mention samādhi. Dhamma is often taught, however, without any mention of samādhi at all. For example, neither the Buddha's second or third sermons mention samādhi, yet both led the audience to arahantship.[34] How should this be understood?

51   Elsewhere, Dhamma is taught with no mention of wisdom. For example, the famous verses known as the 'Exhortation in the Code of Conduct' primarily focus on virtue, but include two phrases indicating meditation: 'brightening the mind' and 'higher mind'. These refer specifically to samādhi. Vipassanā constitutes the 'higher understanding' not mentioned here. Having taught only virtue and samādhi, the Buddha sums up by saying: 'This is the dispensation of the Buddhas.'[35] Are we to understand that wisdom is a dispensable part of the Buddhist path? Or are we better off

---

[32] I have heard anecdotal evidence that seems to confirm this possibility.
[33] MN 43.14, AN 5.25
[34] SN 22.59, SN 35.28
[35] DN 14.3.28; cp. MN 128.32, AN 7.65

remembering the principles of interpretation we have relied on throughout?

52   The Soṇadaṇḍa Sutta exemplifies how these and similar
contexts should be interpreted. A brahman tells the Buddha:

53   'Understanding is purified by virtue, and virtue is
purified by understanding; where one is, the other is;
a virtuous person has understanding, and an understanding person is virtuous; and the combination of
understanding and virtue is called the highest thing
in the world.'

54   'But, brahman, what is that virtue, what is that understanding...?

55   'Here, a disciple goes forth [as in the Sāmaññaphala
Sutta]... undertakes the virtues... guards the senses...
develops mindfulness and clear comprehension... is
content, etc. That, brahman, is virtue.

56   'He enters and abides in the four jhānas... develops
the direct knowledges... and attains the evaporation
of the poisons... That, brahman, is understanding.'[36]

57   When the path is taught in brief, certain aspects may be
emphasized or others omitted to suit the situation. However,
the detailed explanation of these brief teachings should be
given in terms of the overall framework. If jhānas are not
specifically mentioned, they can be included under wisdom.

58   Modern vipassanā schools warn that samādhi leads to
attachment. There seems to be a deep fear of pleasure underlying this doctrine. But the theme finds no support in the
suttas. The 'danger' in samādhi is treated identically with
the 'danger' in mindfulness and understanding; that is, they
are not yet the final goal.[37] Abandoning the subtle relishing
of the bliss of samādhi—reckoned as the fetters of lust for

---

[36] DN 4 condensed.
[37] SN 48.2–7

form and the formless, and in the craving, the poison, and
the inherent compulsion for existence—is chiefly the task
of the non-returner.[38] The issue of attachment to samādhi
is addressed in the following analysis by Venerable Mahā
Kaccāna of an enigmatic statement of the Buddha.

59   'A monk should scrutinize in such a way that as
he scrutinizes his consciousness is not distracted and
scattered externally, is not stuck within, and by not
grasping he is not anxious. If he does so, then there is
no production of birth, aging, death, and the origin of
suffering for him in the future.'...

60   'How, friends, is consciousness called "distracted
and scattered externally"? Having seen a visible form
with the eye, a monk's consciousness follows after the
feature of visible form, is tied, shackled, and fettered
by the fetter of gratification in the feature of visible
form. [And so on.]

61   'And how is consciousness called "not distracted and
scattered externally"? Having seen a visible form with
the eye, a monk's consciousness does not follow after
the feature of visible form, is not tied, shackled, and
fettered by the fetter of gratification in the feature of
visible form. [And so on.]

62   'And how is the mind[39] called "stuck within"? Here,
a monk... enters and abides in the first jhāna. His consciousness follows after the rapture & bliss born of
seclusion, is tied, shackled, and fettered by the fetter
of gratification in the rapture & bliss born of seclusion.
[And so on for the "rapture & bliss born of samādhi"
of the second jhāna; the "bliss with equanimity" of the

---

38 See e.g. Iti 3.96.
39 Here Venerable Mahā Kaccāna switches from 'consciousness' to 'mind'.
Although generally having the same denotation, the suttas tend to
treat 'consciousness' in terms of the first noble truth—'to be fully
known'—and 'mind' in terms of the fourth noble truth—'to be developed'.

third jhāna; and the "neither pleasure nor pain" of the
fourth jhāna.]

63   'And how is the mind called "not stuck within"?
Here, a monk ... enters and abides in the first jhāna.
His consciousness does not follow after the rapture
& bliss born of seclusion, is not tied, shackled, and
fettered by the fetter of gratification in the rapture &
bliss born of seclusion. [And so on.]'[40]

64   Venerable Mahā Kaccāna's exposition is typically subtle
and precise. The three kinds of scrutiny correspond with the
threefold training. The first kind is closely linked with sense
restraint, an aspect of virtue. Note that 'mental phenomena'
are here treated as external to consciousness, just as the
other sense objects. The section on samādhi then follows as
the natural sequel to virtue. The analysis shows that the way
beyond attachment to spiritual bliss is not by avoiding jhāna.
The monk 'not stuck within' practices jhāna just the same,
but uses the subtle wisdom empowered by samādhi to avert
attachment. The suttas consistently recommend samādhi as
part of the practice to overcome attachment to samādhi.[41]

65   Like so many of the suttas, this text is pointing to a gradual
development. First one overcomes the scatterdness of the
mind, which is accomplished through samādhi. Without the
bliss and stillness of samādhi, it is impossible to withdraw
the mind from the clamor of sense activity. Next, only after
one has achieved this, one needs to move beyond the stillness
of samādhi. The text presents this with the stock phrase, 'by
not grasping he is not anxious'. The analysis of this phrase,
which I have not included in the translation above, explains
how, if the five aggregates are conceived in relation to a 'self',

---

[40]   MN 138
[41]   See e.g. MN 8.14.18, MN 113.21*ff.*

anxiety arises when they change. This deep level of insight follows on, as usual, from the development of samādhi.

66 The sutta does not comment on the final phrase: 'The production of birth, aging, death, and the origin of suffering in the future.' However, the identical phrase occurs in the Mahā Nidāna Sutta. There it refers to the fixation of consciousness in mentality & physical form. It suggests the dual role of consciousness, as the center of lived experience and as the sense of identity flowing on in rebirths. The verse which follows the same introductory summary in the Itivuttaka confirms that rebirth is the issue.[42]

67 This ties up with the Bodhisatta's famous rejection of his former teachers under whom he reached the highest formless attainments. When the Bodhisatta first practiced with these teachers, he began by studying the doctrinal theory. This is not explained in detail, but would certainly have placed the practice of samādhi within a conceptual framework, probably positing the eternal existence of a blissful soul in the plane of rebirth corresponding to the samādhi attainment. Any samādhi which results from such a wrong view is of necessity wrong samādhi.

68 The Bodhisatta nevertheless credits his teachers with possessing faith, energy, mindfulness, samādhi, and understanding (here these are not called 'spiritual faculties'), disposing of any idea that mindfulness and understanding are unique to Buddhism. As well as understanding kamma and rebirth, these teachers may well have pointed out that almost everything is impermanent, suffering, and not-self, clinging only to a rarefied view of self.

69 But the Bodhisatta set out on his spiritual quest in search of what was not subject to birth, aging, and death, and so he

---

[42] Iti 3.94

rejected this wrong samādhi of the sectarians, which leads only to rebirth in exalted planes of existence. His respect and gratitude for his former teachers is evident however, since they were the first people he thought of teaching after his enlightenment; having long had 'little dust in their eyes' they would quickly understand the Dhamma. He did not extend the same honor to the self-mortifiers of the group of five monks as he did to the samādhi practitioners, merely commenting that 'they were very helpful'.[43]

70   It is interesting that when the Bodhisatta, immediately before his enlightenment, reflected on his past practice of samādhi, he skipped over his experience with the sectarian teachers, recalling instead an isolated episode from his youth when he sat under the rose-apple tree and attained first jhāna. This memory showed him that samādhi need not be imprisoned within a dogmatic metaphysical framework, but in its essence is simply a natural expression of the gracious flow of the Dhamma.

Conclusion

71   In summary, the passages that have been used to throw doubt on the necessity for jhāna consist of minor doctrinal statements and background stories. Even if we were to find a direct statement of the superfluity of jhāna in such material, could this outweigh the great mass of clear teachings on the path? Better try to derail a freight train with a toothpick. And of course, there is no such direct statement. The Buddha would hardly have fixed jhāna squarely in the heart of the

---

[43] MN 26.22*ff.*

path only to about face and declare a path of all head, no heart.

72   We should never forget that causality is a central features of the Dhamma, underlying the analysis of both the existential problem and the practical solution. The specific factors of the path, functioning as necessary conditions for their specific results, exemplify specific conditionality of phenomena in general, that is, dependent origination. Suggesting that one of the path factors may be optional introduces a fuzziness to the path, retreating from a causal to a correlative paradigm. The path becomes merely a collection of skillful means, not an embodiment of universal principles. It is true that some practices, such as the ascetic practices, formless attainments, and psychic powers are useful but not essential. But these do not occur in the wings to enlightenment or the dependent origination; they are not key factors of the path in the sense under consideration here.

73   Playing around with the key path factors unleashes a host of theoretical difficulties. If one path factor is optional, what of the others? Perhaps there might be more than one path? Then how many? How are the many benefits of jhāna accomplished without jhāna? How to overcome sensuality when one cannot withdraw from the senses? How to overcome restlessness when the mind is still moving? How to transcend concepts when the mind is still labeling? How to perceive subtle truths with coarse consciousness? If one can go beyond hindrances with bare mindfulness, why can't one simply center the mind and go into jhāna? What is hindering jhāna if not the hindrances? Being unable to realize the preliminary samatha of jhāna, how can one realize the ultimate samatha of Nibbana?

74   Deleting jhāna from the path would take more than pointing to a few suggestive passages; it would require a comprehensive model of the path to account for such difficulties.
This is why the doctrine of a path without jhāna was only
developed in the Theravāda school many centuries after the
Buddha, and did not gain prominence until our own times.
That is how long it took to work out a new set of interpretations and explanations that allowed the theorists to sys-
tematically explain away all the very many statements on
the centrality of jhāna to the Buddha's path. But, as I have
shown again and again, that commentarial model is not reliable, and it frequently contradicts the sutta passages it is
purporting to explain. Anyone who wants to dispense with
jhāna needs a new paradigm.

Conclusion:
Unity & Diversity

'"This Dhamma is for one with samādhi, not for one without samādhi." So it was said. For what reason was this said? Here, a monk... enters and abides in the first jhāna... second jhāna... third jhāna... fourth jhāna.'

— THE BUDDHA, AN 8.30

THE BUDDHA NEVER DIVIDED the themes of meditation into two classes: samatha and vipassanā. Nor did he divide meditators into two classes: the samatha practitioners and the vipassanā practitioners. He taught the development of the mind for the ending of suffering. As mind is diverse, so too are the means of development diverse. But if we freeze these different means into different paths we fracture the organic unity of the Dhamma. Some may walk to the left, some to the right; some faster, some slower; some with ease, some with difficulty; but the path itself is one.

> 'This [eightfold path] is the only path
> There is no other for the purification of vision.'[44]

---

[44] Dhp 274

3   I am well aware that by insisting that jhānas are necessary for liberation I court the risk of being labeled intolerant. Many, rightly wary of the specter of religious fanaticism, seek common ground between religions or between branches of the same religion by claiming that surface differences, arising as valid responses to the circumstances of time and place, mask an underlying unity.

4   I believe this is mistaken. Certainly, the Buddha flat-out denied that his teaching was the same as any other. While many differences do indeed float only on the surface, in my opinion an honest appraisal shows that, among many similarities, some meaningful differences persist even in the deep structures of religions—in their philosophies, in the experiences of their sages, and in the sayings of their founders. But of course, non-identity does not mean complete separation or contradiction; it means distinct but related.

5   Anyway, mere tolerance is a stingy virtue. We should do more than tolerate, we should celebrate goodness wherever we find it. We should rejoice in whatever peace, wisdom, and fulfillment any spiritual practitioner finds in their chosen way. We should be happy to live together, talk together, and practice together in a spirit of mutual respect, mutual harmony, and mutual support even if we have differing views or practices.

6   Saying: 'We should get along with them because, in the end, they're the same as us' is perhaps the most intolerant view of all. We value others because they measure up to our standard; but we should value others because of their intrinsic worth, because they measure up to their own standard. More importantly, one treats the truth shabbily. Truth is one, and does not bow to the whims of fashion. Here, surely,

all would agree. The rich diversity of religious and philosophical doctrines in the world are attempts to represent that truth.

7   The view that 'It's all the same in the end' is just one more view. But it is a view perilously intolerant of reasoned inquiry. Declaring sensitive issues out of bounds for fear of disputes is the surest way to sap religion's vitality, relegating it to stagnation and irrelevance. A reasoned, thoughtful critique grants those views the dignity of attention, and it grants the adherents of those views the dignity of taking part in such an inquiry. Investigation can distinguish between trivial and important differences of opinion, and clear the way for meaningful reconciliation.

8   'Disputes about livelihood or the code of conduct are trifling, Ānanda. But should disputes arise in the Sangha about the path or the way of practice [the thirty-seven wings of enlightenment], they would be for the harm and misfortune of many.'[45]

9   'Only this is right—everything else is stupid': this is one extreme view. 'It's all the same in the end': this is a second extreme view. The Buddha taught us to avoid these extremes through analysis and inquiry: 'What is the same? What is different?'

10   In all the deserts on this broad earth there are not even two grains of sand that are completely identical. Still less are there two grains of sand that are utterly different. The true basis of compassion and respect is not a supposed identity of beliefs or paths, but our shared nature as sentient beings. We all feel pain. We are together in this lifeboat earth, drifting on the trackless seas, longing for a glimpse of land.

---

[45] MN 104.5

11   As we share our sorrows, so too we share our joys. And of all joys, none compares with the joy of letting go. This joy belongs to no-one, lives in no country. It is not 'Buddhist', and was not invented by the Buddha. Jhāna is not a difficulty or problem that we should fear, it is a promise that the spiritual life leads to an astonishing pleasure.

12   'One should know how to define bliss, and knowing that, one should pursue bliss within oneself." So it was said. For what reason was this said?

13   'The bliss and happiness that arise dependent on the five cords of sensual pleasure is called the bliss of sensual pleasure—a filthy, coarse, ignoble bliss. I say that this bliss should not be cultivated, should not be developed, should not be made much of, but should be feared.

14   'Here, a monk, quite secluded from sensual pleasures, secluded from unbeneficial qualities, enters and abides in the first jhāna... second jhāna... third jhāna... fourth jhāna. This is called the bliss of renunciation, the bliss of seclusion, the bliss of peace, the bliss of enlightenment. I say that this bliss should be cultivated, should be developed, should be made much of, and should not be feared.'[46]

15   As I emphasized at the beginning, meaning does not inhere in a text. Still less can it be extracted and distilled into a definitive, universal formula. Rather, it arises in the response of the reader. Each reader will respond in their own way. This does not mean that textual analysis is irrelevant, since in some cases we can eliminate misleading readings, and in some cases possible interpretations can be confirmed by experience. But we should always remember that Dhamma does not stop short with the written word.

---

[46]   MN 139.9; cp. MN 66.19–21.

16   'What, Bhante, does "abider in Dhamma" refer to?'

17   ... 'Here, a monk studies the Dhamma—the suttas, songs, expositions, verses, inspired sayings, "so it was said" sayings, birth stories, marvelous teachings, and catechisms.[47] He does not waste his days with that Dhamma he has studied, he does not neglect retreat, he is devoted to samatha of the heart within. Thus, monk, a monk is an "abider in Dhamma".

18   'Thus, monk, I have taught you the monk who studies a lot, the one who teaches a lot, the one who recites a lot, the one who thinks a lot, and the one who abides in Dhamma. I have done for you what should be done by a Teacher seeking the welfare of his disciples out of compassion. Here, monk, are roots of trees, here are empty huts. Practice jhāna, monk! Do not be negligent! Do not regret it later! This is our instruction to you.'[48]

19   Dhamma is no weekend pastime. A crash course in meditation cannot be expected to effect any substantial, lasting transformation. If we want quick results we are likely to end up either disappointed or deluded. But if we allow our lives to yield to the soft touch of the Dhamma, our minds will grow more and more peaceful as our attachments grow less and less. Samatha is not about trying very hard to scale some far-off mountain peak; it is about being content with the wholesome happiness of the present moment. This is beyond no-one's reach. We usually underestimate the task; but we underestimate our own potential even more.

20   'I thought of a time when my Sakyan father was working and I was sitting in the shade of a rose-apple tree, where quite secluded from sensual pleasures, secluded from unbeneficial qualities, I entered and

---

[47] These are the nine *aṅgas* into which the Buddhist texts were classified before the development of the *nikāya* system.

[48] AN 5.73

abode in the first jhāna, with initial & sustained application of mind, and the rapture & bliss born of seclusion. I thought: "Might that be the path to enlightenment?" Then following up that memory there came the awareness:

"That indeed is the path to enlightenment."[49]

[49]   MN 36.31, MN 85, MN 100

Appendix A

On the Translations

IN THE INTERESTS OF READABILITY and concision I have
taken some liberties with condensing and paraphrasing the
translations, and have divorced the chosen passages from
their original contexts. On the other hand, I have treated
doctrinal terms and passages with rigorous consistency, occasionally falling back on that last resort of the inept translator—word for word literalism. I have frequently relied
on earlier translations, particularly the wonderful works of
Bhikkhu Ñāṇamoḷi and Bhikkhu Bodhi, but the final choice
of rendering is in all cases my own. I have retained the Pali
terms for the crucial meditation terminology in all occurrences, with the exception of *satipaṭṭhāna*, which I have
occasionally rendered 'establishing of mindfulness'. Otherwise, Pali has been retained only for a few words probably
more familiar to Buddhists than their English equivalents—
arahant (accomplished one), *vinaya* (discipline), *sādhu* (it is
good!), *bhante* (venerable sir), *saṁsāra* (course of rebirths).
I have generally dispensed with capitals for doctrinal terms

as being justified neither by the Pali nor by current English. Since words such as *sutta*, *vinaya*, and *abhidhamma* may have a less specialized meaning in early Pali, I capitalize only when unambiguously referring to actual texts.

2   Following is an explanation of my approach to some of the technical terminology.

3   **Anusaya** is the most fundamental level of the defilements, which, even if not presently active, will inevitably manifest when the conditions are ripe. 'Tendency', on the other hand, refers to a mere inclination. I have used 'inherent compulsion'.

4   **Avakkanti** is usually rendered following etymology as 'descent', but it seems more sensible to follow the unambiguous contextual meaning in dependent origination and elsewhere of 'reincarnation'. The contexts should clarify that this refers to a conditioned stream of consciousness, not an eternal soul.

5   **Āsava** has been rendered 'poison' rather than the feeble 'taint', which has been used for *upakkilesa*.

6   **Upanisā** has been derived by scholars from *upanisīdati* (so the subcommentary), or from *upanissāya* (so the commentary). The former supports the rendering 'proximate condition', the latter 'vital condition'. 'Virtue is the *upanisā* for samādhi' is an often-repeated, idiomatic usage of the term; but the proximate condition for samādhi is not virtue but bliss. *Upanisā* can substitute for *paccaya* as a general term for 'condition'; but its most idiomatic usage is in the dependent liberation, and there it means primarily 'vital condition'. We have met *upanisā* with this meaning in the definition of right samādhi at MN 117.1, etc. At AN 9.1 good friendship, virtue, talk on wanting little, etc., energy, and understanding are said to be the *upanisās* for the develop-

ment of the wings to enlightenment. Similarly, at AN 3.67, lending an ear (to listen to Dhamma) is an *upanisā* for direct knowledge, etc. These too are both necessary[1] and, as the passage emphasizes, strongly inducive, but not proximate, conditions. I therefore take this as being the basic meaning, applied with some flexibility in other contexts.

7   ***Kāya*** usually means 'body', but in samādhi the five senses that make up the body have disappeared. The formless attainments, the deathless, the ultimate truth,[2] and cessation are said to be contacted 'with the *kāya*'. This last also rules out the '*nāmakāya*' (mentality body). At DN 27.9, *kāya* is synonymous with '*bhūta*': 'has become dhamma, become holy'. In other expressions also, for example the '*kāya*-witness',[3] *kāya* emphasizes the directness of personal engagement. This meaning fits well in the samādhi contexts, so I have used 'person' or 'personally'. On the other hand, the '*kāya*-tranquility' that occurs before samādhi is surely parallel with the stage of breath meditation consisting of 'tranquilizing the *kāya*-activities'. This is the in-and-out breaths, and so refers simply to the physical body.

8   ***Khaya*** is gentler than 'destruction', which is handled by other words in the Pali. It means 'drying up' (of a stream), 'using up' (of supplies), 'waning' (of the moon), etc. I have used 'evaporation'.

9   ***Dhamma*** has been left untranslated, or rendered with 'principle', 'quality', 'phenomenon', or 'teaching', rather than 'state', which is precisely what it is not. Bhikkhu Bodhi rather curiously asks us to accept the rendering 'state' divested of both its chief denotation—the existing condition of a per-

---

[1]   Buddhas notwithstanding—the context is the training for disciples!
[2]   MN 70.23
[3]   E.g. AN 9.43; see also SN 48.50 quoted above, SN 48.53

son or thing—and connotation—staticity (MLDB, p.54). This rendering reinforces the ontological concretization of the concept of *dhamma*.

10   *Nipaka* (adjective) or **nepakka** (noun) appear most prominently as part of the compound *satinepakka* in the definition of mindfulness as spiritual faculty, etc. The resemblance of this compound to *satisampajañña* (mindfulness and clear comprehension) may have influenced the commentaries to gloss *nepakka* with 'understanding'. But other contexts show a closer connection with the Sanskrit cognate meaning 'chief, master'.

11   'You should abide with the doors of the sense faculties guarded (*gutta*), with mindfulness protected (*ārakkhasati*), with masterly mindfulness (*nipakasati*), endowed with protected mind, with heart protected by mindfulness.'[4]

12   The meaning as 'mastery over the senses' also applies in the sequence virtue, *nipaka*, satipaṭṭhāna at MN 51.3, and at Snp 144. As a quality of a good friend (Snp 45, Snp 283) *nipaka* means 'self-mastery, self-control'. *Nipaka* is a quality of samādhi at AN 5.27 (quoted above), and in the compound *ekodinipaka* at SN 1.290 and Snp 962. Here too it means mastery:

13   'With constant virtue, masterly (*nipaka*), in jhāna
       Whose mind is mastered (*vasībhūta*), one-pointed in samādhi
    That wise one, scattering the darkness
       With the threefold realization, is destroyer of Death.'[5]

14   *Nimitta* in the suttas never means 'radiant reflex image in meditation'. This was referred to rather as 'light and vision

---

[4]   AN 5.114
[5]   AN 3.58

of forms', the 'radiant mind', etc. The commentarial usage of *nimitta* for this light is possibly influenced by such passages as this.

15   'When, good sirs, the *nimittas* are seen, illumination is born, and light manifests, then Brahma will manifest.'[6]

16   At AN 5.193 the various pollutants and disturbances to water, compared with the five hindrances, prevent one from seeing 'the *nimitta* (reflection) of one's own face'. The commentarial term 'apprehending sign' (*uggaha nimitta*) was possible derived from passages such as AN 6.68 and SN 47.8; but here the meaning seems to be 'apprehending the character of the mind', how the mind responds to various 'foods'. AN 6.68 shows that 'apprehending the *nimitta* of the mind' is a preliminary stage of meditation, before fulfilling right view and then right samādhi. In at least some meditation contexts *nimitta* just means 'cause'.[7] It refers to some quality, aspect, or feature of experience which, when paid attention to, promotes the growth of a similar or related quality. This meaning fits in well with the contexts in this work, so I have adopted the rendering 'basis' rather than 'sign', which does not carry a causal implication. AN 3.19 says that a monk who does not 'carefully resolve' on their *samādhi nimitta* (here = meditation subject, perhaps satipaṭṭhāna) in the morning, midday, or evening cannot grow in good qualities. At MN 128.28 the phrase 'I pay attention to the light-*nimitta*' occurs, but even here I would regard the term 'attention' as hinting at a causal implication, consistent with the usage in the sutta.

---

6   DN 19.15
7   At SN 48.40 *nimitta* = *nidāna, saṅkhāra, paccaya*, and at MN 128.16 *nimitta* = *hetu, paccaya*.

17   **Rūpa** refers to the physical world as it appears to the mind. It includes energy, the *tejodhātu*, and is thus broader than 'matter' or even 'materiality'. The rendering 'physical form' attempts to capture both the breadth and the subjectivity of *rūpa*, and retains the connection with *rūpa* as the objects of sight, 'visible forms'.

18   **Vitakka** and **vicāra** do not mean 'thinking' in the context of jhāna. Thinking involves a succession of different mental objects and therefore cannot apply to the still one-pointedness of jhāna. Jhāna is a state of altered consciousness, and it is only to be expected that psychological terms will take on new and more refined meanings. The following passage brings out this distinction.

19   'I understood thus: "This thought (*vitakka*) of renunciation... non-ill will... non-cruelty which has arisen does not lead to the affliction of myself, of others, or of both. It matures understanding, relieves stress, and leads to Nibbana. But if I think on and consider on (*anuvitakka, anuvicāra*) for too long, my body will be strained. When the body is strained the mind is stirred up, and a mind stirred up is far from samādhi." So I steadied, settled, unified, and concentrated my mind in samādhi within myself. For what reason? So that my mind would not be stirred up...

20   '... My energy was roused and unflagging; my mindfulness established and unconfused; my body tranquil and relaxed... I entered and abode in the first jhāna, with initial & sustained application of mind (*vitakka, vicāra*).'[8]

21   Further, mindfulness of breathing is taught for cutting off thinking (*vitakka*),[9] and at MN 20 five methods for quelling

---

8   MN 19
9   Ud 4.1

thoughts are taught; both of these practices are for the development of the higher mind, i.e. jhāna, including the jhāna factor of initial application (*vitakka*). If this implicit distinction is embodied in the translation, there is no need for the underivable rendering of *vitakka* in such contexts as 'distracting thoughts'. All thoughts, even thoughts about the Dhamma,[10] must be abandoned for the mind to find peace.

22   ***Vossaggārammaṇaṁ karitvā*** is interpreted by the commentaries as meaning 'taking Nibbana as the object [of the mind in samādhi]'. This is identified as the transcendental samādhi of the noble path (moments) and fruits. Apart from our general critique of the concept of the momentary path, there are several reasons to doubt such an interpretation. Normally the Pali absolutive—here signified by 'having'—expresses a subordinate action completed before the main action of the sentence. This is the regular verb form in phrases at the start of the jhāna formula to signify the ending of the obstructions to jhāna or the fulfillment of the qualities leading to jhāna. For example: 'quite secluded from sensual pleasures' or 'having abandoned these five hindrances'. The sentence: '*Idha bhikkhave ariyasāvako vossaggārammaṇam karitvā labhati samādhiṁ labhati cittass'ekaggataṁ*' is syntactically straightforward, so there is no reason to propose any non-standard interpretation. Compare the formula for the bases for psychic powers: '*Chandaṁ ce bhikkhave nissāya labhati samādhiṁ, labhati cittass'ekaggataṁ...*' The commentarial explanation, however, entails the simultaneous occurrence of the main action with the subordinate clause. This may just be grammatically possible (almost any grammatical rule can admit some exceptions), but hardly likely. Bhikkhu Bodhi (CDB, p.1930), perhaps in-

---

[10] AN 3.100, AN 5.73

fluenced by the commentary, takes *vossaggārammaṇaṁ kar-itvā* in apposition to 'samādhi' (grammatically the patient of the sentence, in accusative) rather than 'noble disciple' (the agent, in nominative). This is certainly unusual; Warder (*Introduction to Pali*, p.48) lists no such usage of the absolutive.

23   The phrase may be compared with the passage on the development of the six recollections: 'Having made this the support (*idaṁ ārammaṇaṁ karitvā*), some beings here are purified.'[11] Here, *ārammaṇaṁ karitvā* is obviously in apposition to 'beings', the agent. This passage also gives a good idea as to the meaning of *ārammaṇa* as 'support' or 'basis'; the previously developed good qualities that underpin further development. A related usage occurs at MN 21.11—one develops loving kindness towards one person, and then, relying on that (*tadārammaṇaṁ*), towards all beings. In such contexts the meaning approaches 'meditation subject'. This meaning is probably intended in the (late?) Jhānasaṁyutta.[12] From here, perhaps, developed the usage of *ārammaṇa* as 'object (of consciousness)', dominant in the abhidhamma but absent from the suttas, on which the commentaries rely to interpret *vossaggārammaṇaṁ karitvā*.

24   There are other difficulties with the commentarial explanation. The definitions of some of the other spiritual faculties, for example that of mindfulness as 'memory of what was said and done long ago', has nothing to do with any 'path moment'. The commentaries therefore resort to a convoluted division of the spiritual faculties as transcendental, nontranscendental, and mixed. This directly contradicts the suttas that restrict the spiritual faculties to the noble indi-

---

[11]   AN 6.26, quoted above.
[12]   SN 34.5. Incidentally, should not *gocara* at SN 34.6 mean satipaṭṭhāna, the meditator's 'native habitat'? (see SN 37.6).

viduals. Also, since 'transcendental' samādhi occurs before 'non-transcendental' understanding, it makes nonsense of any notion of progressive development.

25   **Saṅkhāra** has an active meaning in most of its occurrences, so I have reflected this by rendering it as 'activities' rather than 'formations'. This preserves the link with its etymological sibling 'action' (*kamma*), for which it often serves as a substitute. *Saṅkhāras* as the second link of dependent origination and the fourth aggregate are defined as volition (*cetanā*). However, particularly as the fourth aggregate, the abhidhamma takes them to be broader than that, encompassing a wide range of mental phenomena, from basic functions like contact to sophisticated emotions like equanimity. While the rendering 'conceptual activities' is too narrow for this, it is broader than 'volitional activities', and it emphasizes the conceptual, linguistic functions that are most typical of this aggregate, as well as the pregnant, causative aspect.

26   **Sacchikaroti** has been rendered by the literal 'witnessing', thus preserving the connection with 'personal witness' (*kāyasakkhi*), and freeing up 'realization' for *vijjā* rather than the tautologous 'true knowledge', in turn enabling 'knowledge' to be consistently reserved for words based on the root *ñāṇa*.

Appendix B

Contemporary Teachers on Samādhi

'Right samādhi as the last link of the eightfold path is defined as the four meditative absorptions [jhānas].'

BHIKKHU ÑĀṆATILOKA
Buddhist Dictionary

'... the suttas themselves say nothing about a system of bare insight meditation...'

BHIKKHU BODHI
The Connected Discourses of the Buddha

'The Pali Piṭaka explains right samādhi in terms of the four jhānas.'

MAHASI SAYADAW
A Discourse on Sallekha Sutta

'The eightfold path includes both right view and right samādhi. A person who is to gain release has to develop all eight factors of the path. Otherwise they won't be able to gain release.'

Pra Ajahn Mun Bhūridatta
A Heart Released

'Wisdom is the fruit of samatha.'

Pra Ajahn Chah Bodhiñāṇa
A Taste of Freedom

'According to the suttas, concentration of jhāna strength is necessary for the manifestation of the path.'

Bhikkhu Ñāṇamoli
Path of Purification (Visuddhimagga), introduction note 21.

'Wisdom and samādhi are a "dhamma pair" which go together and cannot be separated.'

Pra Ajahn Mahā Bua Ñāṇasampanno
Wisdom Develops Samadhi

'The wisdom that can let go of defilement is a special wisdom, not ordinary wisdom. It needs samādhi as its basis if it's going to let go.'

Pra Ajahn Fuang Jotiko
Awareness Itself

'The wisdom of vipassanā is not something that can be fashioned into being by arrangement. Instead, it arises from samādhi that has been mastered until it is good and solid.'

Pra Ajahn Thate Desaraṁsī
Buddho

'If the mind goes running around without stopping, it doesn't really see suffering. It has to be still if it wants to see.'

PRA AJAHN LEE DHAMMADHARO
The Skill of Release

'The four jhānas are invariably included in the complete course of training laid down for disciples. They figure in the training as the discipline in higher consciousness, right concentration of the Noble Eightfold Path, and the faculty and power of concentration.'

DR HENEPOLA GUNARATANA
A Critical Analysis of the Jhānas in Theravāda Buddhist Meditation

Appendix C

Instant Enlightenment

IT ALL SEEMS SO EASY. Sit worshipfully at the feet of an all-enlightened Buddha, allow the rapture of devotion to suffuse one's mind, and rely on the Buddha to know just the right time to implant the seed of Awakening. No need to worry about meditation, renunciation, ethics. The idea of instant enlightenment has been used to justify a number of theses, past and present, all of which I feel distort the main orientation of the Buddha's teachings as recorded in the Nikāyas/Āgamas, viz:

1) That jhāna is not necessary for realizing the Dhamma

2) That the path is ultimately just a mind-moment.

3) That attainment of the Dhamma is only possible due to the direct personal instruction of a Buddha.

4) That in our degenerate times it is impossible to realize the Dhamma.

The teachings on instant enlightenment in the Pali canon do not provide substantial support for any of these views.

Further, there are many features of such episodes that suggested that many of them are late interpolations.

7   1) The texts that prominently feature such episodes tend to be late

8   2) The frequency of such episodes increases steadily with the passing of time

9   3) Some of the events are intrinsically implausible

10   4) They are usually just background stories, typically not attributed to or confirmed by the Buddha.

11   5) Anyone can remember where a discourse was given and what was said, but few are able to reliably assess transcendental attainments.

12   The comparative study of the Pali suttas with texts of other traditions throws further doubt on these passages. Here are a few examples of the kinds of differences that we typically find in the accounts of attainment realized during a Dhamma talk. This is not a detailed study, just a few notes I have taken from Thich Minh Chau's *The Chinese Madhyama Āgama and the Theravāda Majjhima Nikāya*.

Ākaṅkheyya Sutta (MN 6/MA 105)

13   MA 105 ends with the monks going into seclusion, striving, and attaining arahantship. MN 6 says nothing of this. (CMA & PMN p.227)

Vatthūpama Sutta (MN 7/MA 93)

14   At the end of MN 7, the brahman Sundarika Bhāradvāja went for refuge, asked for ordination, and later, after striving, attained arahantship. In MA 93 he merely went for refuge and remained a lay follower. (CMA & PMN p.232)

Upāli Sutta (MN 56/MA 133)

15   In both versions, Upāli, the wealthy supporter of the Jains, was converted by the Buddha and in the same session, while

the Buddha taught him the gradual training, he attained the vision of the Dhamma. (CMA & PMN p.285f.)

Māgandiya Sutta (MN 75/MA 153)

16   In MA 153 Māgandiya, a wanderer of another sect, was initially critical of the Buddha, was converted by him, experienced the vision of the Dhamma, went forth, and after striving attained arahantship. MN 75 omits the arising of the vision of Dhamma, but the other main elements are similar. (CMA & PMN p.62)

Vekhaṇassa Sutta (MN 80/MA 209)

17   MA 209 is similar to MA 153 above. Vekhaassa was initially critical of the Buddha, was converted by him, experienced the vision of the Dhamma, went forth, and after striving attained arahantship. However, MN80 simply reports that Vekhaassa went for refuge as a lay follower. (CMA & PMN p.62)

Raṭṭhapāla Sutta (MN 82/MA 132)

18   In both versions Raṭṭhapāla goes forth, strives, and attains arahantship. (CMA & PMN p.294ff.)

Poṭaliya Sutta (MN 54/MA 203)

19   In MA 203 the householder Poṭaliya attained the vision of the Dhamma during the discourse, then went for refuge as a lay devotee. MN 54 omits the arising of the vision of the Dhamma and is content to have Poṭaliya go for refuge. (CMA & PMN p.71)

Brahmāyu Sutta (MN 91/MA 161)

20   Both suttas agree that Brahmāyu, a learned and venerable brahman, attained the vision of the Dhamma during the discourse, died soon afterwards, and the Buddha declared that he had become a non-returner. The Chinese betrays its sloppy editing here by having Brahmāyu rejoice in the

closing statement of the Buddha, even though he's already dead! (CMA & PMN p.311ff.)

Bakkula Sutta (MN 124/MA 34)

21   Acelakassapa asks his former friend Venerable Bakkula a rather personal question and receives in reply an account of Venerable Bakkula's high attainments and rigorous asceticism. In MN 124 he asks for the going forth, strives, and attains arahantship. MA 34 omits these details. This suggests that the Theravāda may have emphasized a more ascetic, solitary mode of practice than did the Sarvāstivāda. (CMA & PMN p.75)

Dhātuvibhaṅga Sutta (MN 140/MA 162)

22   In MA 162 Pukkusāti is said to have attained the vision of the Dhamma during the discourse. However MN 140 omits this, saying that, after hearing the discourse and asking for the going-forth, Pukkusati was killed by a cow and the Buddha declared that he was a non-returner. The Theravāda commentary, however, also says that Pukkusati attained the vision of the Dhamma during the discourse, thus agreeing with the Sarvāstivāda version. This agreement might be held to suggest that this was an early tradition passed down in the Theravāda community but for some reason not included in the canonical account. On the other hand, bearing in mind that the commentary has greatly elaborated the background story to this sutta, this may simply be one of a number of stock details that are commonly inserted in the stories of great disciples. (CMA & PMN p.70)

Chachakka Sutta (MN 148/MA 86)

23   MN 148 claims that 60 monks became arahants while listening to this discourse. MA 86 is silent. The Theravāda commentary further exaggerates the episodes of instant enlight-

enment at subsequent preachings of this discourse, confirming the impression that the Theravādins were anxious to exalt this proto-abhidhamma style analysis. (CMA & PMN p.206)

24   Thus, of all the statements concerning the attainments of particular individuals, three are the same (Upāli, Raṭṭhapāla, and Brahmāyu) while the remaining eight are different. Of those, if we focus on the statements that refer specifically to attainment while listening to a discourse, two are the same (Upāli and Brahmāyu), while five are different (Poṭaliya, Māgandiya, Vekhaṇassa, Dhātuvibhaṅga, Chachakka). This correlation of around 30% should be compared with the near identity of key doctrines such as the four noble truths, the noble eightfold path, and the dependent origination. Even a trivial detail such as the settings of the suttas shows around 80% correlation. Also note that the only two discourses that agree in attributing the vision of the Dhamma to a new disciple while listening to a discourse are two of the most obvious propaganda vehicles in the whole canon. The Upāli Sutta was delivered to a wealthy chief disciple of the Jains (and we need not be surprised to find this story of the last days of the Jain teacher Mahāvīra as recorded by the Buddhists does not agree with the accounts in the Jain literature). The Brahmāyu Sutta was delivered to one of the most revered elders of the brahmans.

25   Bearing this in mind, together with the considerations I advanced at the start of this essay, I conclude that the historical reliability of the records of attainment in the Majjhimas approximates to zero. This does not mean that such events cannot happen—the mind is a strange and wonderful place. But we should be exceedingly cautious before drawing any inferences about the Dhamma based on the assumption that

any particular incidents of instant enlightenment are literal historical fact.

Abbreviations

Pali texts

DN	Dīgha Nikāya
MN	Majjhima Nikāya
SN	Saṁyutta Nikāya
AN	Aṅguttara Nikāya
Dhp	Dhammapada
Ud	Udāna
Iti	Itivuttaka
Snp	Sutta Nipāta
Thag	Theragāthā
Vin	Vinaya
Cv	Cūḷavagga
Mv	Mahāvagga
Pj	Pārājika
Vsm	Visuddhimagga
DNA (etc.)	Dīgha Nikāya Aṭṭhakathā (etc.)

Chinese Āgamas

MA	Madhyama Āgama (Taishō no. 26)

Translations

LDB	Long Discourses of the Buddha (Walshe)
MLDB	Middle Length Discourses of the Buddha (Ñāṇamoḷi, Bodhi)
CDB	Connected Discourses of the Buddha (Bodhi)

References to the suttas are to *sutta* and section of LDB and MLDB; *saṁyutta* and *sutta* of CDB (which varies from the reckoning in earlier texts and translations, especially in SN 35), or verse number for the Sagāthāvagga; to *nipāta* and *sutta* for the Aṅguttara Nikāya and the Itivuttaka; *vagga* and *sutta* for the Udāna; and verse number for the Dhammapada, Sutta Nipāta, and Theragāthā.

Having ordained in Thailand in 1994, Bhante Sujato returned to his home town Perth in 1997 to practice in Bodhinyana Monastery under Ajahn Brahm. In 2003 he became the abbot of Santi Forest Monastery. He has published a series of books and articles, and in addition has been actively involved in helping re-establish the order of nuns. Currently he is translating the four Pali nikāyas to be published on SuttaCentral.